D1500148

The Kentucky Bicentennial Bookshelf
Sponsored by

KENTUCKY HISTORICAL EVENTS CELEBRATION COMMISSION
KENTUCKY FEDERATION OF WOMEN'S CLUBS

and Contributing Sponsors

AMERICAN FEDERAL SAVINGS & LOAN ASSOCIATION
ARMCO STEEL CORPORATION, ASHLAND WORKS
A. ARNOLD & SON TRANSFER & STORAGE CO., INC. / ASHLAND OIL, INC.
BAILEY MINING COMPANY, BYPRO, KENTUCKY / BEGLEY DRUG COMPANY
J. WINSTON COLEMAN, JR. / CONVENIENT INDUSTRIES OF AMERICA, INC.
IN MEMORY OF MR. AND MRS. J. SHERMAN COOPER BY THEIR CHILDREN
CORNING GLASS WORKS FOUNDATION / MRS. CLORA CORRELL
THE COURIER-JOURNAL AND THE LOUISVILLE TIMES
COVINGTON TRUST & BANKING COMPANY
MR. AND MRS. GEORGE P. CROUNSE / GEORGE E. EVANS, JR.
FARMERS BANK & CAPITAL TRUST COMPANY / FISHER-PRICE TOYS, MURRAY
MARY PAULINE FOX, M.D., IN HONOR OF CHLOE GIFFORD
MARY A. HALL, M.D., IN HONOR OF PAT LEE,
JANICE HALL & MARY ANN FAULKNER
OSCAR HORNSBY INC. / OFFICE PRODUCTS DIVISION IBM CORPORATION
JERRY'S RESTAURANTS / ROBERT B. JEWELL
LEE S. JONES / KENTUCKIANA GIRL SCOUT COUNCIL
KENTUCKY BANKERS ASSOCIATION / KENTUCKY COAL ASSOCIATION, INC.
THE KENTUCKY JOCKEY CLUB, INC. / THE LEXINGTON WOMAN'S CLUB
LINCOLN INCOME LIFE INSURANCE COMPANY
LORILLARD A DIVISION OF LOEW'S THEATRES, INC.
METROPOLITAN WOMAN'S CLUB OF LEXINGTON / BETTY HAGGIN MOLLOY
MUTUAL FEDERAL SAVINGS & LOAN ASSOCIATION
NATIONAL INDUSTRIES, INC. / RAND MCNALLY & COMPANY
PHILIP MORRIS, INCORPORATED / MRS. VICTOR SAMS
SHELL OIL COMPANY, LOUISVILLE
SOUTH CENTRAL BELL TELEPHONE COMPANY
SOUTHERN BELLE DAIRY CO. INC.
STANDARD OIL COMPANY (KENTUCKY)
STANDARD PRINTING CO., H. M. KESSLER, PRESIDENT
STATE BANK & TRUST COMPANY, RICHMOND
THOMAS INDUSTRIES INC. / TIP TOP COAL CO., INC.
MARY L. WISS, M.D. / YOUNGER WOMAN'S CLUB OF ST. MATTHEWS

The County in Kentucky History

ROBERT M. IRELAND

THE UNIVERSITY PRESS OF KENTUCKY

Research for The Kentucky Bicentennial Bookshelf
is assisted by a grant from the
National Endowment for the Humanities.
Views expressed in the Bookshelf do not
necessarily represent those of the Endowment.

ISBN: 0-8131-0229-4

Library of Congress Catalog Card Number: 76-4436

Copyright © 1976 by The University Press of Kentucky

A statewide cooperative scholarly publishing agency
serving Berea College, Centre College of Kentucky,
Eastern Kentucky University, The Filson Club,
Georgetown College, Kentucky Historical Society,
Kentucky State University, Morehead State University,
Murray State University, Northern Kentucky University,
Transylvania University, University of Kentucky,
University of Louisville, and Western Kentucky University.

Editorial and Sales Offices: Lexington, Kentucky 40506

Contents

Preface

NINETEENTH-CENTURY Kentucky in many ways resembled medieval Germany, which was essentially a loose collection of miniature states, duchies, principalities, and other constitutional subdivisions and only in the loosest sense a political unit. Although Kentucky certainly possessed stronger bonds of central control, her essential governmental functions were in many ways conducted not from Frankfort but from the seats of her multitudinous counties (numbering 119 by 1886). Often the county rather than the state or national government controlled the destinies of Kentuckians, regulating their affairs from apprenticeship to probate. County officials likewise mimicked medieval bureaucrats, often assuming a proprietary attachment to their offices.

By 1900, Kentucky led the country in the production of race horses and whiskey and placed near the top in tobacco, coal, and counties. Counties served well the passions of Kentuckians for individualism, local control, economic gain, and, above all, political power. The full story of Kentucky cannot be understood without an appreciation of the place of the county in her past.

Many people contributed to this book. In particular, I wish to thank Dr. Steve Channing, Dr. Thomas D. Clark, Mr. Paul Willis, Mr. Sandy Gilchrist, and Dr. Jacqueline Bull. Above all I want to thank my three children, Suzy, Julie, and Betsy, for keeping biting and fighting to a minimum during the period of my writing. To them I affectionately dedicate this book.

1

THE STAKES
OF POWER

KENTUCKIANS HAVE ALWAYS taken great pride in their counties. This was especially true before 1900 when most Kentuckians lived on farms or in rural towns and villages and owed their greatest allegiance to local institutions such as family, church, political party, and state and local government. For most, Washington, D.C., remained a distant capital and the nation a remote loyalty even after the Civil War. In an age of relative immobility, "home" had a more permanent and meaningful hold on the hearts and minds of Kentuckians. And for most Kentuckians, "home" meant one's county rather than his town or village.

Kentucky's preoccupation with counties was natural to the child of a parent so concerned with the invention and perfection of these local institutions. More than most colonies, Virginia had depended upon counties for her government, delegating to these entities the principal responsibility for tax assessment and collection, law enforcement, military training, and many of the other fundamental devices of social control. After a period of turmoil approaching rebellion, the leaders of Virginia's counties had become the leaders of the colony. To be a county squire in seventeenth- and eighteenth-century

Virginia was to be at the top of the social and political ladder.

Kentucky, once the westernmost county of Virginia, assumed the traditions of local government from that colony. Early in her statehood, Kentucky displayed a particular predilection for the art of county-making which did not abate as the decades passed. By the end of the nineteenth century, Kentuckians had created 119 counties, adding still another in the early twentieth century. Originally intended to be but subdivisions of the state and, as such, her agents in local affairs, most of Kentucky's counties had become semiautonomous by the mid-nineteenth century, deriving a fierce loyalty from their residents. Rivalries between counties could be as intense as those between states.

At first most of Kentucky's counties were created because settlers found it difficult to reach county seats not within one day's travel from home. But by the third decade of the nineteenth century, entrepreneurs and politicians had begun to influence the formation of new counties. The response of citizens of the southern part of Mercer County in and around Danville was typical. They became so chagrined with the policies of the Harrods-burg-dominated county government that in 1834 they began to petition for a new county. Danvillians accused the Mercer County Court of overtaxation, fraudulent elections, and discriminatory fiscal planning. Disagreement over national politics compounded their frustration, the Danville crowd favoring the Whigs while their counterparts in Harrodsburg generally supported the Democrats. After eight years of petition and counterpetition, in which the dissidents advocated constitutional secession, the legislature finally authorized the divorce of the south from the north with the formation of Boyle County.

Land speculators often lurked behind proposals to form new counties. An enterprising farmer in Trigg County petitioned the legislature shortly after the Civil War to form a new county out of his farm and part of neighboring

Marshall County. While the petitioner's stated purpose was to honor his daughter Henrietta (by naming the county after her), detractors accused him of trying to convert his infertile farm into a county seat and sell off town lots at inflated prices. The opposition prevailed, first defeating the proposal at a special election and then throttling the measure in the General Assembly.

Rivaling the intensity of battles over the creation of new counties were contests over the location of county seats. Once a county seat was established it usually was not moved, but neighboring towns often attempted to secure the political and economic benefits accruing to such governmental centers by obtaining legislative permission to hold special referenda on the question of relocation. Maysville successfully engineered such a campaign in 1848, despite the efforts of Washington, Mason County's first county seat, to prevent a move. More typical was the indecisiveness of the commissioners who established Lee County in 1870. Unable to agree on the location of a county seat, they left it up to the voters at a special election. When Beattyville was chosen over Proctor, distressed Proctorites went so far as to seek legislative abolition of the new county rather than give in to the decision of the voters.

Kentuckians desired to live in new counties and county seats because of the rich political and economic rewards involved. A position in county government often meant monetary as well as political riches. The county court formed the nucleus of county government. Until 1850, the court was composed of the justices of the peace, who dispensed much of the local political patronage as well as performing a wide variety of significant governmental business. Although an individual justice of the peace commanded little in the way of income from fees, as a member of the county court he often profited from the sale of county office.

Theoretically, the governor appointed the justices of the peace—approximately fifteen per county. But normally he abided by the recommendations of the county court justices themselves, who were bound to submit two nominations to him for each vacancy. Traditionally the governor selected the court's first choice unless the candidate was morally grotesque. If a justice of the peace sat on the court long enough to become the senior justice, he usually became the sheriff, since the county court controlled nomination to this office as well; the court nominated two candidates for the sheriffalty to the governor from among the members of the court itself, paying due regard to seniority, and the governor almost always commissioned the senior justice of the court.

Before 1850, county courts appointed most of the other officers of the county directly, without outside approval. In addition to dispensing patronage, county courts sat as the probate courts for the commonwealth, maintained jurisdiction over orphans and apprentices, tried bastardy cases, administered the poor laws, established ferries and set their rates, and authorized the construction of milldams. Perhaps most important, the county court and other county officers set the county levy and collected both county and state taxes. They also authorized the construction of many of the state's roads and maintained most of them. The court also paid the county's bills, sitting as a claims court for this process. Much of this may sound like routine business, but the nineteenth century specialized in limited government, and in Kentucky much of what was done by government was accomplished at the county level.

Constitutional reformers at mid-century established the office of county judge, assigning him much of the business previously conducted by the justices of the peace collectively. The justices retained a limited position on the court, sitting once or twice a year as a claims court, which continued to set local taxes and supervise the construction and maintenance of roads and public buildings. The county judge probated wills, heard petty

4

civil and criminal cases, and generally looked after the judicial business of the county court.

Neither county judges nor justices of the peace had to be trained in the law—and few of them were. Statistical studies reveal that in the 1850s most justices of the peace were farmers, with a scattering of artisans, small businessmen, and lawyers. In rural counties county judges tended to be farmers, while in more urban areas they were more likely to be businessmen or, in a few cases, attorneys. Throughout the nineteenth century, observers complained about the caliber of justices of the peace. Before 1850, the justices generally found themselves in the upper half of the community's society and economy, but performed their duties less than conscientiously. Such dereliction helped produce the reforms of 1850. After mid-century, the typical justice of the peace came from a lower socioeconomic stratum than before and executed his official duties even less competently. It was sometimes said that not even God himself could guess how a justice of the peace would decide a case. Often devoid of legal logic, rulings of the justices sometimes bordered on the bizarre. A Franklin County squire, upon learning of the innocence of a man he had ordered whipped for horse-stealing, said, "It's all right—the fellow needed the thrashing anyhow." Another justice ruled for both parties in a trespass suit, while a colleague dissolved a marriage in the middle of a wife-beating trial so that the wife could testify against her husband. Still another forced a would-be wife to swear off other men before marrying her to her suspicious suitor.

County judges maintained higher standards, although some in smaller, poorer counties could not read or write. Yet eccentric behavior sometimes characterized these officials also. Benjamin F. Graves, for many years county judge in Fayette County, remarked when awakened from one of his frequent courtroom naps that he could hear as well asleep as awake. The judge of the Kenton County

5

Court created a monopoly in civil marriages by refusing to grant the justices of the peace in his county the authority to compete with him. When accused by counsel of favoritism, a Bullitt County judge left the bench, soundly thrashed his accuser, voluntarily appeared before a justice of the peace to be fined for disorderly conduct, and then resumed the trial.

The sheriff's office, with its infinite responsibilities, grew increasingly frustrating to occupants and clients alike as the nineteenth century matured. The sheriff collected county and state taxes, executed the orders of the commonwealth's principal trial courts, served as chief election officer of the county, and held primary responsibility for law enforcement. He also sometimes acted as a court-appointed estate administrator. In larger, more prosperous counties, the office of sheriff could be one of great profit and prestige, but in smaller, poorer places it often represented a position of small income and great chagrin. In economically stable counties, tax collecting offered the greatest opportunity for sheriffs to earn substantial fees in the form of commissions, but it also presented the greatest hazard in the form of suits by the commonwealth and county for delinquencies. Large numbers of Kentuckians (up to 25 percent in some counties) evaded taxes, and sheriffs remained liable for much of their delinquency. Furthermore, the job of tax collecting was a great deal more cumbersome than it is today; sheriffs in most counties were forced to ride horseback from household to household, personally collecting from each taxpayer. Sheriffs from various counties sometimes banded together to protest inadequate commissions and antiquated collection methods, but partial relief came only in the latter decades of the nineteenth century. Until then, legislatures simply delayed the day of final reckoning by postponing dates upon which sheriffs had to settle their accounts with the state auditor and providing other forms of temporary relief. One legislature made the mistake of providing that counties could appoint special tax collectors in the event the sheriff neglected his duties; because these collectors could charge higher commissions for their services, many sheriffs resigned their positions to secure appointment either as the special tax collector or as his chief deputy.

Traditionally the principal law enforcement officer of the commonwealth, the sheriff gradually came to ignore his crime-fighting responsibilities as his other duties multiplied. Ironically this happened at a time when crime was on the increase, and thus semianarchy resulted in many counties, especially during and after the Civil War. Those sheriffs who did participate actively in law enforcement often did so in a fraudulent manner, stage-managing collusive crimes of a petty nature in order to earn state fees for the apprehension and jailing of his accomplices. In many feud-ridden communities sheriffs either refused to confront armed gangs or themselves joined and even led the desperadoes. In either case, local crime fighting became a mockery and governors had to restore order by means of the state militia.

The county clerkship normally attracted more competent occupants than the sheriffalty. The clerk of Jefferson County reportedly earned $15,000 annually by 1850. But in smaller counties it was usually necessary to secure an additional appointment as clerk of the circuit court in order to obtain a living wage. In smaller counties clerks also sometimes engaged in the practice of law, attempting to exploit the inherent advantages of their office. Legislatures attempted to outlaw or limit this activity, but enjoyed only incomplete success. By the second half of the century, clerks found their jobs so complex that they began organizing to seek legislative clarification and simplification of their duties, again with only partial success.

The other officers of late eighteenth-century and nineteenth-century Kentucky county government performed more in the tradition of justices of the peace and sheriffs, being generally less competent than county judges and clerks. Jailers tended to be far more interested in earning fees than in holding their prisoners secure. Even in smaller counties, the position was one of potentially sizable profit because of the high incidence of crime. Jailers earned fees not only from the county, but from state and federal governments as well. Some jailers supplemented their official income by selling liquor to prisoners, and a few collaborated in jail escapes in return for pay-offs. Many in smaller counties maintained outside occupations in addition to their official duties. A few jailers qualified as genuine humanitarians; in Kenton County one such officer left his trade as a blacksmith in order to care for a sickly prisoner.

The offices of assessor and county attorney normally attracted younger men eager for political advancement. Their ambition and inexperience sometimes caused them to perform less than effectively. This was especially true of the assessors, who often underassessed in order to curry favor from voters. Supporters of the county attorneys argued that their assistance often proved invaluable in successful criminal prosecutions by commonwealth attorneys, but most observers concluded that defense attorneys generally possessed superior abilities in the courtroom.

Though possessed of a rich English tradition, the offices of coroner, surveyor, and constable steadily declined throughout the nineteenth century. The first two became a joke in many counties and often went unfilled. Few physicians aspired to coronerships, and those who did were not infrequently accused of body-snatching. Once an avenue to successful land speculation, the surveyorship languished by mid-century and often attracted only fledglings eager to bolster inadequate private practices. Theoretically law enforcement officers, constables actually devoted most of their time to harassing debtors and defendants. But at least until 1850, an enterprising constable could bolster his annual income considerably by virtue of the fees he earned from his official debt-collecting.

Even before the injection of popular democracy into the selection process, politics played a major part in the appointment of county officers. For most of the period before 1850, the county court in effect picked not only its own members, but virtually all other county officials as well. Thus vacancies on the courts themselves inspired much of the politicking. Although spirited battles for these positions took place before the two-party system came to Kentucky in 1827, competition afterward was even keener. In many cases the question of which party would control a particular county court was determined almost immediately after organized political activity coalesced around the candidacies of Andrew Jackson and John Quincy Adams early in 1827 as a prelude to the presidential election of 1828. And it sometimes happened that the political party controlling a county court was not the one polling the most votes in the popular elections of the county.

In Fayette County, for example, Jacksonian Democrats, though largely unsuccessful at the ballot box, dominated the county court. This control originated largely by chance. In 1827 the Jacksonians happened to have a majority on the court. During the next four years they took care to bolster their narrow majority by filling all vacancies on the court with members of their own party. By 1831, the anti-Jacksonian newspapers of Lexington were condemning the county court as "an irresponsible body of aristocrats." Despite the denunciations and pleas for more bipartisanship, the situation had not changed by 1845; of twenty-two justices, only three were members of the Whig party. Democrats enjoyed similar successes in other counties that usually voted Whig, such as Franklin, Montgomery, and Woodford, while in Jacksonian Harrison County the Whigs dominated the court.

Sometimes party struggles over the control of county courts raged for several decades. Democrats did not seize control of the Campbell County Court until 1840, and it took a rump session of the county court for them to accomplish this feat. Despite protests from his fellow Whigs, Governor Robert Letcher acquiesced in the Democratic coup. Seven years later the Whigs exacted a measure of revenge when they foisted one of their own party members upon the Democratic majority in the guise of a follower of the Jacksonian banner. But the Democrats quickly retaliated the following year by securing the appointment of a blazing partisan in the face of accusations by Whigs that he was not only capable of making prejudicial rulings as a magistrate, but also quite insane.

"Out" parties often attempted to lessen "in" party domination of county courts by means of petitions to the governor bolstered by the endorsements of mass meetings. Sometimes dissidents demanded special referenda to fill county court vacancies even though the constitution and statutes did not require such a procedure. Public demonstrations seldom influenced court appointments, however, and when they did they sometimes produced surprising results. In 1843, Mason County Whigs dominated both the county court and the ballot box. Confident of victory, they agreed to the demands of Democrats and held a special election to determine a particular neighborhood's choice to fill a vacancy on the court. Much to the dismay of the Whigs, a Democrat, strongly challenged not only by a Whig but also by another Democratic candidate, triumphed over all opposition. The Whig majority on the court quickly forgot its pledge to abide by the outcome of the referendum and in the face of howls from the Democrats filled the vacancy with a fellow party member.

Not all political battles over county court vacancies involved party politics. Since there was no requirement that every section of a county should have membership on the court, geographical malapportionment plagued many county neighborhoods. The problem was especially acute in Logan County. When the senior magistrate of the county court resigned in 1845 to become sheriff, residents of an unrepresented region petitioned the court to fill the vacancy from their neighborhood. Not only did the court ignore the pleadings of the aggrieved district, but it also delayed filling the vacancy until the retiree's term as sheriff expired and then reappointed him to the court.

Chicanery likewise characterized the appointments of other county officers, especially sheriffs, clerks, and constables. The tradition of awarding the sheriffalty to the senior member of the county court encouraged another antebellum Kentucky tradition—the selling of public office. In the words of a newspaper of the time, a sheriff-designate had to be equipped "to be moving continually on horseback, or on foot, in all sorts of weather, over all sorts of roads, and sometimes at night, as well as during the day." By the time a justice of the peace reached a position of seniority on the court he was often too old and feeble for such a strenuous life. The senior magistrate of Henry County, asserting that he was "quite an old man and in a very feeble state of health and apprehending that he [would] live but a short time," sold the sheriffalty to a deputy in 1843, and this was not an unusual case.

Profit likewise influenced many senior justices to sell the sheriffalty. Although illegal, such sales often took place at public auctions with the office going to the highest bidder, regardless of his place of residence, for as much as $4,000. In early 1846, a combination of businessmen from Montgomery County known as "Richart, Anderson and Company" purchased the sheriffalty of Bourbon County one year in advance of commission. When the time came in early 1847 for the buyers to assume control of the sheriffalty in the person of their senior partner, Richart, they appeared in the Bourbon

County Court with their lawyer and demanded that the incumbent sheriff and his deputies surrender all unfinished business. When the court refused to grant the purchasers' request, they threatened to bring suit in the circuit court. The group secured the office despite complaints from county residents that Richart was "superannuated" and predictions that he would "clog the wheels of litigation" and fail to enforce the laws.

Political entrepreneurs also bought and sold the offices of county clerk, deputy sheriff, and constable. Of these the clerkship brought the highest prices, ranging from more than $10,000 in populous Jefferson County to less than $1,000 in smaller counties. As in the case of sold sheriffalties, law enforcement officers seldom if ever prosecuted parties to such transactions even though they patently violated criminal statutes. The only recorded litigation took the form of civil suits to enforce sale and leasehold agreements, some of which resembled complicated real estate transactions. In 1816, John D. Young, clerk of the Fayette County Court, leased his office to Abner Fields for one year at a price of $1,000. Before the end of the period of the lease, Young sold the office to James C. Rodes for $6,000. Rodes thereupon paid the lessee, Fields, $400 in the form of eight $50 notes in return for the latter's promise to execute all the business of the clerk's office until the expiration of his lease. Fields assigned some of the notes to Thomas Outon, and when Rodes refused to satisfy them, Outon sued him and won a judgment. Rodes then sought to enjoin enforcement of the judgment on the grounds that Fields had failed to perform the duties of his office. The Court of Appeals refused to issue an injunction because the original contract was against public policy.

Kentucky's antebellum county politicians did not reserve all of their shenanigans for appointment battles; fights over removals also claimed a good share. Some county offices were not protected by constitutional or statutory guarantees of definite tenure; the jailership, for example, remained vulnerable to political attack because of vague statutory language. Scheming politicans eagerly preyed upon incumbents who blocked their path to patronage and power. One such episode occurred in Franklin County in 1845 and 1846.

Predictably the conflicting ambitions of local politicians sparked the Franklin County jailership donnybrook. Benjamin Luckett, a member of the county court, applied for a deputy postmastership of Frankfort, placing himself in competition with several other party members of the county. In order to remove Luckett from this competition and to speed up the process of succession to the sheriffalty (Luckett had considerable seniority on the county court), Luckett's colleagues on the court offered to appoint him jailer if he resigned from the court and withdrew his application to the post office. Although Luckett agreed to this, the incumbent jailer, Thomas A. Gorham, did not. Probably the Democratic majority on the court did not even consult Gorham, who was a Whig. Scarcely affording Gorham an opportunity to defend his office, the county court abruptly removed him from office in June 1845 for "divers good causes." Gorham appealed to the Court of Appeals, which ruled the county's action invalid on the grounds that the jailer was entitled to a full hearing.

Undaunted by the seeming reversal of their carefully laid plans, the county magistrates refused to enter the high tribunal's ruling in their order book, and Luckett would not give Gorham back the key to the jail. After several months of hesitation, the Court of Appeals jailed almost half of the Franklin County justices for contempt of court, while the Whig legislature, not to be outdone, passed a statute making the usurpation of office a crime. Unfortunately for the Whigs and Gorham, the offending Franklin County magistrates were confined in Mr. Luckett's jail. After residing there for several days, they petitioned each other for writs of habeas corpus and, after

13

brief hearings marked by more tittering than argumentation, ordered Luckett to free them on the grounds that they were being held in jail contrary to law. Gorham completed the farce by suddenly resigning the jailership he no longer held, thus allowing Luckett and the Franklin County Democracy to evade the decrees of the highest court of the commonwealth and a statute of the General Assembly.

The democratic revolution of 1850 that made almost all county offices elective did not alter local Kentucky politics significantly. The sale of office gave way to the sale of votes. Voting continued to be done by voice rather than ballot until the end of the nineteenth century, making it a simple matter to enforce agreements to vote for particular candidates. It was common for candidates to employ professional vote-buyers to round up voters at strategic moments on election day. Sometimes professionals brought in wagonloads of voters from other counties, although such practices obviously were illegal. The smart vote-seller waited until a close election neared completion and then sold his vote for a much higher price than it would have commanded earlier in the day. Prices for votes ranged from two to fifty dollars. Candidates also employed large amounts of liquor in their quest for office, and some floated to victory. Grayson County Republicans enjoyed unprecedented success at the polls in 1886 when they rented an entire saloon on election day. Prohibitionists in Clark County sought to counteract drinking at the polls by providing voters free ice cream.

Vast quantities of free liquor and the often intensely competitive nature of many county elections meant that many election days were the scenes of drunken brawls, maimings, and even killings. Newspaper correspondents expressed surprise when they could report no deaths or serious fights on election day. A reporter in Spring Lick wrote that the whole town was drunk and disorderly during the elections of 1882. Obviously such outrages produced demands for modern-day laws against the sale of alcoholic beverages on election day.

Drafters of the Constitution of 1850, while providing that county officials should be elected, did not specify how they should be nominated, and critics began to complain after the Civil War that the traditional method of party nomination by convention rendered the democratic revolution incomplete. Most charged that popular primaries furnished the only method of insuring that the people had a direct voice in the selection of local officials. Under the prevailing system, they maintained, political bosses, tricksters, and so-called courthouse cliques controlled the nominating process. Conventions lent themselves to orators and wire-pullers and attracted few but sordid professionals; primaries would give every voter an equal opportunity to influence nominations. In one-party counties (there were a good number of these following the Civil War), those who determined nominations decided who would be county officers.

Defenders of the old order countered that popular primaries would be unmanageable, affording an opportunity for members of the opposition to infiltrate the polls and influence the nomination. Such dissidents would certainly opt for the weakest candidate. What damage they did not do would come at the hands of the general riffraff who would participate in primaries as a lark. Furthermore, primaries would produce divisiveness within party ranks and allow minority candidates to run in the general election. Cries of cliques, rings, and bosses were simply the exaggerations of "out" politicians trying to get into power.

Those favoring popular primaries generally prevailed in the battles over nominating procedures which afflicted many counties after the Civil War, and many of the evils forecast by critics of primaries materialized. In Pendleton County's primary of 1878, the local newspaper reported that scores of outsiders and opposition party members voted and that candidates using the most money and dispensing the most whiskey emerged victorious. Similar scenes in other places prompted parties in some counties to secure special legislation from the General Assembly authorizing them to regulate primaries more closely and to impose criminal sanctions on violators of party rules. Finally, in 1892, the legislature enacted a law regulating party primaries wherever held.

Controversy over methods of nomination did nothing to dampen the traditional Kentucky fervor for politicking and the seeking of political office. Observers noted an obsession motivating hordes of persons to seek county office who "would not otherwise descend into the cesspool of politics." In the opinion of the *Boone County Recorder,* many sought office "in the hope of being aided in providing for their families by the salaries paid these offices." Ironically, the paper noted, the least lucrative offices seemed to attract the greatest number of candidates. Reporting from Green County, a correspondent wrote that most of the candidates for county office in 1878 emphasized their need for sustenance rather than their qualifications for office. Appalled by the mad scramble for office, the *Kentucky Gazette* of Lexington denounced the tendency of candidates for county office to conduct prolonged campaigns, some of which lasted over a year. But such condemnations did little good, and nineteenth-century Kentuckians remained dedicated to their favorite pastime—politicking.

Although cynics, especially those tied to the establishment, often branded talk about "cliques" and "rings" as the myth-making diatribes of "out" politicans trying to get into power, the county courthouse gangs of the nineteenth century were more than mere figments of the imagination. County officers, especially justices of the peace and sheriffs, held positions of party leadership in many counties during the period of the first and second state constitutions. After 1850, the relative power of county officers within county political machines declined, but certain members of the county government nonetheless remained influential. Candidates for elected office especially catered to the sheriff, who as chief election officer and enforcer of civil and criminal judgments could be very persuasive at the polls. And after the office of county judge was created in 1850, these officials obtained considerable political power and often commanded the unofficial title of "political boss" of the county, a position many maintain even to this day. In short, counties constituted not only the governmental foundation of nineteenth-century Kentucky, but its political base as well.

2

SOCIAL ORDER

A GREAT MANY ASPECTS of the daily lives of nineteenth-century Kentuckians fell under the regulation of county governments. As the exclusive probate courts of the state, county courts annually controlled millions of dollars of property. Critics accused the courts of negligence and even fraud in the handling of estates. Courts took too long to distribute property, they said, stalling settlements in order to extract exorbitant fees for themselves and their cronies whom they installed as administrators and appraisers. Many contestants in probate conflicts found it necessary to appeal rulings of the courts to higher tribunals, but such actions afforded little effective relief and mainly served to prolong disputes. At both constitutional conventions held in the nineteenth century, efforts to transfer probate jurisdiction from the county courts to special tribunals failed despite continued criticism.

In an age of high mortality, the court's jurisdiction over guardians and orphans affected thousands of homeless children, some with rather large holdings that needed protection and supervision. Yet for all their potential as conservators of these often helpless waifs, the tribunals too willingly acquiesced, either through negligence or collaboration, in the thievery of unscrupulous guardians.

Akin to their powers over guardians and orphans was county governments' jurisdiction over masters and apprentices. The relationship of master and apprentice is unfamiliar to modern Americans, but it was a vital part of nineteenth-century society; apprenticeship was by far the most popular way of training youth in skilled trades. County courts had to approve indentures of apprenticeship and reserved the right to fine or remove negligent or repressive masters. Thus the courts in a real sense comprised the most important judicial overseer of labor relations in nineteenth-century Kentucky.

So, too, the farmer and miller went to the county court for permission to construct milldams for the gristmills where most of Kentucky's grain was ground in the nineteenth century. As the agency in charge of licensing and regulating milldams, the counties considered not only the potential effects of dams on neighboring property but also rudimentary questions of ecology. Since the county court also had jurisdiction over poaching, it was in many ways the most effective instrument of conservation in the commonwealth.

In the absence of federal or even state programs (except for the handicapped), health and welfare concerns resided almost exclusively in the counties. Counties were the principal administrators of the nation's poor laws well into the twentieth century. What little concern governments had for health matters manifested itself most often at the county level. County courts issued emergency decrees during epidemics of smallpox and cholera, and many eventually established departments of health to look after the more routine needs of their citizens. Whenever their business concerned estates, apprenticeships, guardianships, relief of the poor, or milldams, nineteenth-century Kentuckians depended on their counties for assistance and guidance. And these concerns were a vital part of the authority of nineteenth-century government.

Court day likewise highlighted the economic and social importance of counties in nineteenth-century Kentucky. Originally a Monday devoted primarily to governmental and judicial business, court day evolved into that day of the month during which most county residents shopped, bought and sold, bartered, drank, gossiped, fought, and competed in various athletic contests. County courts continued to convene on court day, but their business contributed in diminishing degree to the day's festivities.

In central Kentucky especially, court day became the day on which most of the region's livestock was sold. Famed Kentucky author James Lane Allen contended that the area was "the great livestock market of the West." Farmers herded their livestock onto roads and turnpikes and, amidst swirling clouds of dust, drove them to court day auctions. In some county seats, especially Lexington, the occasion attracted so many animals that city residents began to demand restrictions on, or even elimination of, the sales.

Paris in Bourbon County (where the stock sales apparently originated) and Lexington were the principal stock centers of the Bluegrass. As was typical of such events, Lexington's court day also attracted countless other commercial and social activities, and by the end of the Civil War it was a scene of animated chaos. Producing a stench that reportedly could cause "a strong, well man" to vomit as he walked the streets, the livestock accounted for most of the growing complaints about Fayette County court day. On rainy days the animals, together with the thousands of human onlookers, turned muddy streets into quagmires. Women dared not venture too far from the shops they frequented for fear of being shouldered about by the teeming crowd. Gathering for the most part in the public square on Cheapside, the "nuisance" of the livestock had become a "calamity" by 1870 and produced a clamor for restrictions. Some residents demanded that the city construct pens in the public square; others argued for better traffic control (it was not unusual for two or more large herds to meet head-on); and more and more advocated moving the sales outside of town.

Early in that year, the city of Lexington reluctantly agreed to experiment with suburban livestock sales. Declining profits soon prompted downtown merchants to demand a return of the sales to Cheapside, and by the end of the year the city fathers had restored the old system. Nonetheless, agitation for a permanent removal of the sales—and the "peculiar and pungent ammonia" they created—continued throughout the decade. Ultimately the city council outlawed downtown cattle and hog auctions; although Cheapside merchants once more complained about declining sales, the change remained permanent.

Horsemen found court day greatly to their liking. In all counties residents swapped horses, and in many they conducted formal sales and shows. Fayette County boasted the most elaborate display of horses and was especially noted for fine trotters. By 1870, the Lexington show attracted horsemen not only from all parts of the United States but from the rest of the world as well. Races also contributed to the excitement of this and other shows and ranged from informal, impromptu dashes to more carefully staged affairs. Unlike other events of court day in Lexington, the Fayette County horse show continued well into the twentieth century and its offspring thrives even today.

Livestock dealers were not the only ones conducting business on court day. Entrepreneurs of all kinds flocked to county seats on this day of the month. Among others, patent medicine men, lightning rod salesmen, bookmen, and lumber dealers could be seen eagerly hawking their wares on street corners, in the middle of sidewalks, or in the thick of drifting crowds. Perhaps most important in the vast array of salesmen was the auctioneer, whose barking added to the day's cacophony and whose wares ranged from livestock and real estate to furniture and slaves. Kentuckians conducted so much of their business on court day that it took a Court of Appeals ruling to establish that foreclosure sales were valid even though not held on the traditional Monday.

Court day also represented a major social event, allowing rural and urban residents alike an opportunity to swap the day's news over glasses of punch. Observers noted that democracy characterized the day's socializing, with little attention paid to rank or economic position. Liquor and the Kentuckian's predilection for indiscriminate titling doubtless facilitated this leveling process. A postwar correspondent for the *New York Times* marveled at the number of military officers present at a court day he attended and speculated that it would be easier to find "John Smith in New York City" than "Squire or Judge Somebody in the crowd."

Often intimidated by brawling, drunken men, smelly cows, and sprays of tobacco juice, women found refuge in shops that faced the public square or in nearby churches where they conducted bake sales and public dinners to raise funds for charity. In February 1873, the ladies of a Presbyterian church of Lexington announced in a local newspaper that they wished all of their rural neighbors to remember they could "get a good dinner without detention . . . in Mr. Long's building on the corner of Cheapside and Short Street," while the ladies of a Baptist church held "an elegant dinner" at the April court of the same year.

Would-be athletes frequently gathered on court day to fight, race, or engage in other contests. Competition varied from sledge throwing and bar heaving to foot-racing and cockfighting. Fisticuffs drew the most attention, ranging from spontaneous drunken brawls to staged affairs involving only two contestants and a semblance of refereeing. In some places the intake of alcoholic beverages took on many of the characteristics of an athletic competition. Although counties and towns attempted to restrict its sale and consumption after the Civil War, liquor remained a highly popular item at most court days throughout the nineteenth century.

Drawn by the presence of captive audiences, politicians flocked to court days. They often proclaimed their speeches to be spontaneous responses to popular demands for elucidation of current issues, but court day orators seldom delivered any remarks that had not been carefully thought out beforehand. Those who took the stump usually employed agents to gather crowds, and some even hired claques. Barbecues and burgoos sometimes embellished the politicking. The day also presented an excellent occasion for more formal political meetings such as conventions.

Competition between neighboring counties' court days remained lively throughout much of the nineteenth century. Often the entire economy of a county depended upon the success of the occasion and this in turn usually depended on strategic scheduling. If a county's court day came at the same time as that of a nearby county with more facilities and attractions, economic disaster could quickly result. Finding that their day conflicted with those of Fayette, Nicholas, and Grant counties, officials of Harrison County successfully petitioned the legislature for a change of date (despite the resentment of traditionalists) and happily reported the economic revival that soon resulted. Counties often engaged in bragging contests over the relative merits of their court days. Its neighbors denounced Bourbon County's braggadocio and contended that their own court days were every bit as spectacular. The *Cynthiana News* asserted that Bourbonites actually envied Harrison County and that such envy was well founded, since Harrison's court day excelled in every way except for numbers of "long-eared animals . . . both of quadrupeds and bipeds."

Court day remained popular in most counties throughout the nineteenth century. Occasional flu and cholera epidemics kept attendance down in certain counties, and, of course, the war interfered from time to time in battle areas. But even then, crowds gathered in the public square to exchange the latest news as soon as the noise of battle abated.

The introduction of the automobile signaled the decline and fall of court day as a major institution in the lives of Kentuckians. The event did not die without resistance, anguish, and controversy, however. Fayette County's conflict in the early 1920s best illustrates this painful process. Supported by steady agitation from women's groups and various other organizations of "forward-movers," a grand jury in the fall of 1920 found court day to be a "nuisance" and indicted the city of Lexington for "maintaining" it. In the trial held a year later, a circuit court jury (which included three farmers) found the city guilty, and the judge soon afterward ordered the city "not to permit bartering, trading, selling or dealing in wares, goods, merchandize, mules, horses or any articles" on or in the vicinity of Cheapside, the area of the public square where the main events of court day traditionally occurred. City authorities, most of whom welcomed the decision, announced they would not appeal the order.

Far less acquiescent, the Fayette County Fiscal Court voted to fight the order, contending it was invalid since Cheapside was part of the courthouse square and the county, not the city, owned the square. The grand jury should have indicted the county instead of the city, and therefore the order was ineffectual. The Fayette County Farmers' Union joined the fiscal court's effort to prevent enforcement of the order, declaring that Cheapside was "the only place [farmers] had to do a little business in the city." A spokesman for the union bitterly announced that he now knew what the expression "back to the country" really meant. "It is a hint to the farmers to stay in the country and not bother the city with their presence."

Other farmers alluded to a conflict between town and country in even more direct terms. A neighboring Woodford County farmer, Bill Hayden, in a letter to the *Lexington Herald* described city dwellers as "kid gloved geraniums" and "tenderfoots." Hayden alleged that the farmers of Fayette County and environs accounted for the greatness of Lexington, supporting her retail establishments and developing her most important industries (horses and tobacco). Hayden pictured city dwellers cowering by warm fires while manly farmers braved intemperate weather to harvest crops, breed animals, and make progress. Vowing that the farmers would never give up Cheapside, he urged his city neighbors to "pull together for a better court day and a better market."

Echoing the charge of urban hypocrisy and elaborating upon the theme of town versus country, a rural "citizen" contrasted the alleged "stench" of court day livestock with the "moral stench" of city mores. In his opinion, Lexingtonians should spend less time complaining about the habits of farmers and more time getting rid of "the vamps—male and female—who walk around trying to trap the innocent." So evil was the city that a "citizen" claimed to know a young man who had come to Lexington to study, arriving "a clean boy" and leaving "diseased."

Others took up the cudgel for court day. A newspaper editor from Jessamine County admitted that Fayette County's court day created minor confusion but contended that "a few hours of noisy trafficking" were more than offset by the rich tradition of the event and the contribution of its participants to the city's economy. Seizing upon the economic impact of court day, the Farmers' Union submitted affidavits to the circuit court from several city merchants attesting to the profits they derived from the monthly crowds. Another fundamental issue raised by the court day controversy was mentioned in a letter to the *Herald*. Although a city resident, the writer denounced Lexington's capitulation to the automobile, because of whose reckless drivers people could not "safely walk the streets at all."

Although less vocal, critics of court day rallied to the defense of the grand jury and circuit court. They contended that the event was no longer an occasion for the exchange of farm goods and animals, but had degenerated into "an open market for old junk." Countering the declarations of merchants who saw a profit in court day, some Cheapside residents tesitifed that their property values declined as a result of the monthly gatherings. To these critics, court day represented an outdated tradition, interfering with city life, progress, and, above all, the automobile. They demanded not only that court day be ended, but that Cheapside be converted into a parking lot.

Most city people probably shared the ambivalent attitude of the editorial writer for the *Herald* who characterized court day as "one of the most picturesque and at the same time grotesque features of community life in the Blue Grass." Despite its continuing charm, the journalist pronounced its liabilities excessive. It had "grown beyond governable proportions."

As country and city folk traded shots in the local newspapers and meeting places, some of the principal actors of the drama attempted to resolve the conflict. The Farmers' Union, despite defiant cries from a few of its members urging the fencing off of the public square from the city, instructed its attorney to seek a compromise with the circuit judge, a course of action also endorsed by the county judge, who had been working diligently in behalf of the preservation of court day. The two sides maintained an uneasy truce for more than two years. In November 1924 the county judge himself, weary of the continuing controversy, finally ordered court day discontinued. While some magistrates grumbled about not being consulted and several farmers growled about the demise of their monthly gatherings, the judge's order escaped serious challenge. A rural poet had unwittingly written court day's epitaph several years before while defending the sacred rural institution:

> *Thus, Cheapside, thou art fated,*
> *Old landmark of a time.*

26

> *Ah! Thy prestige stands abated,*
> *Thou'rt accus'd of novel crime.*
> *Behold! Thou art now indicted.*
> *(Stand'st defendant at the bar.)*
> *Alas! Thy fair name's now blighted.*
> *Sullied by the autocar.*

By 1940, court day had all but vanished in most counties. It persisted in some of the more rural areas until after World War II, but by 1960 it existed in only a handful of counties and was usually held only annually and on days not associated with the meeting of the county court.

3

WAR AGAINST
THE CITY

THROUGHOUT THE nineteenth century, Kentuckians remained county-oriented, more loyal to these local units of
government than to towns or to state and national government. Some county-worshipers even advocated abolishing towns as unnecessarily complicating the local constitution. Usually relations between counties and towns
remained harmonious, but occasionally towns bridled
over the domination of counties, which retained more
governing authority under the constitution and statutes.
In a few instances townsfolk obtained important concessions from the General Assembly, and the frustrated
county politicians then staged revolts of their own. Such
episodes occurred within a few months of each other in
Fayette and Jefferson counties.

Although it had lost out commercially to Louisville in
the 1820s, Lexington nonetheless became a semi-inde-
pendent municipal corporation in 1831 by virtue of a
special charter granted by the General Assembly. Chief
among the new city's autonomous features were its separate judiciary and its immunity from county taxation. The
former freed the city fathers from dependence upon the
county for law enforcement, while the latter not only
expanded significantly the city's taxing potential but al-

so eliminated a major grievance that had persisted throughout the period of Lexington's status as a town—namely, that town residents paid taxes to the county without receiving significant benefits. The charter also had other provisions that expanded the powers of Lexington at the expense of Fayette County; the city could, for example, open its own poorhouse, appoint its own food inspectors, and license taverns within its boundaries.

During the next five years, relations between town and country, which had been relatively amicable, deteriorated steadily. Its revenues sagging as the result of Lexington's newly won financial independence, the county court unsuccessfully petitioned the General Assembly in 1833 for a statute that would have applied all fines received by the city court "to the use of the county of Fayette in lessening the county levy." Two years later the city, faced with an early energy crisis, sought to hold down the rising price of wood (upon which its residents largely depended for fuel) by establishing uniform standards of weight and maximum prices. Outraged both by accusations that they were deliberately short-weighting their cords of wood and by the attempts to deny them windfall profits in a period of energy shortage, the farmers of Fayette County petitioned the city government for repeal of the obnoxious wood ordinance. City residents, in turn, held meetings at which they praised the ordinance, denounced the alleged price-gouging of wood sellers, and proposed the incorporation of a municipal fuel company to import wood and coal, making Lexingtonians less dependent on county wood dealers. Undaunted by this consumer revolt, wood sellers held meetings of their own, submitting that their "individual rights" were being denied and threatening to boycott city merchants if the ordinance was not repealed.

Eventually the city repealed the ordinance, but this did not lessen tensions between Lexington and Fayette County. Early in 1836, Thomas Hickey, judge of the

29

Fayette County Circuit Court, precipitated another confrontation between the two units of local government, the seriousness of which greatly exceeded that of the wood controversy. Hickey ruled that the judiciary of Lexington was unconstitutional, on the grounds that the judge was not appointed for life as the state constitution provided. The city charter vested judicial powers in the mayor who was in effect elected for a one-year term. Strangely, no one had bothered to challenge the validity of the municipal court, even though its deficiency seemed obvious, until one Nelson Turner did so in late 1835. Lexington's mayor-judge, James E. Davis, fined Turner, a farmer and resident of the county, fifty dollars for breach of the peace. Rather than pay the fine, Turner went to jail and appealed the decision to the circuit court. Judge Hickey's decision freed Turner and voided the city court's authority.

Stripped of their city court, Lexington officials soon appealed to the General Assembly for relief. The legislature quickly responded to the city's plight, but in a manner so unique that it threatened the very existence of the community as a municipal corporation. Instead of creating a new judicial position, the legislature removed executive responsibilities from the mayor and made him a life-appointed judicial officer. It transferred the mayor's administrative duties to the president of the city council. Governor James T. Morehead then reappointed as mayor his fellow Whig James E. Davis, and the city council promptly elected Thomas Hart, also active in Whig politics and a nephew of Henry Clay's wife, its president.

These developments presented Fayette County Democrats with an opportunity to undermine their Whig opponents and brought to a head the tensions between the two parties and between the separate units of local government. Such tensions resulted naturally from the political complexion of the city and county governments. Taking advantage of their majority at the inception of two-party politics in 1827, Democrats on the county court nominated only fellow party members to fill vacancies, so that by 1836 they maintained almost complete control of the tribunal. All of this particularly galled the Whigs, who maintained a decisive advantage at the ballot box both within the city and in the county at large. As the most popular political party, they naturally controlled the government of Lexington, whose officials were mostly elected rather than appointed. City Democrats, on the other hand, waged spirited battles to overthrow their Whig oppressors and accused them of using fraudulent tactics to win elections. As if to support these accusations, Whigs in 1834 engineered the elimination of ward voting for councilmen in order to minimize Democratic domination of the first ward and further reduce their participation on the council. Thus by 1836, each party controlled a local unit of government and harbored thoughts of revenge against the opposition. Relying on the unpopularity of the city charter's bizarre revisions (which seemed to many to be nothing more than a crude attempt by the Whigs to entrench themselves further in the halls of city government), the Democrats would strike first.

Led by General John McCalla, a party leader on both the county and the state level and a federal marshal since Andrew Jackson's accession to the White House, the Democrats began circulating a petition calling for the complete repeal of the Lexington city charter, a move designed to weaken the Whigs and enhance the powers of the Democratic county court. Simultaneously the editorial cannonades of another prominent Democrat began to be heard. Daniel Bradford, editor of the venerable *Kentucky Gazette* and a member of the county court, was embittered by his recent loss to Davis in the election for mayor and relished the opportunity to lash out at the scheming Whigs. Early in February, Bradford's paper accused the Whigs of conspiring to undermine popular control of the city government and of pocketing city funds; and at the same time the paper endorsed the attempt to repeal the city charter.

After gathering a large number of signatures on their

petitions, Democrats presented them to the legislature, seeking a statute repealing the city charter. The Whig assembly would have none of this, but after some jockeying finally consented to a compromise measure providing for a special referendum by which Lexington voters would determine the fate of the municipal corporation. As the date for the special election approached, both sides intensified their campaigns.

In many respects the issue involved not simply the status of Lexington but the rivalry of city versus county. Whig city fathers could be seen at street corners ardently extolling the virtues of their municipal corporation, while Democratic county officers just as zealously supported the drive to repeal. Midway in the campaign, in another move to embarrass their adversaries, some of the Democrats on the county court sought unsuccessfully to remove Davis from the tribunal on the grounds that he could not be both mayor and justice of the peace at one time. Appointed to the court before the emergence of well-defined political parties, Davis was one of the few Whig members of county government. Whigs correctly branded the maneuver to unseat Davis as blatantly partisan, pointing out that Democrats had tolerated Davis's plural office-holding for more than a year before suddenly deciding it was illegal.

Whigs pointed to other Democratic hypocrisies. Daniel Bradford had earlier opposed an abortive attempt to oust Davis as mayor and to repeal the city charter. Far better, he had counseled, to elect a new mayor at the next election, who would remedy the evils that Davis had allegedly engendered. Not surprisingly, Bradford himself soon thereafter became a candidate for mayor, and at no time in that campaign did he support repeal of the city charter. Bradford had also served as the appointed city clerk throughout 1835, never complaining about the deficiencies of city government and relying almost entirely on his deputy to carry out his official duties. Another leading repealer, Dr. Caleb W. Cloud, had served for many years on the old town board of trustees and later was a member of the city council. In 1822, he had led an attempt to force the county to sell to the town part of the public square (traditionally counties owned the public square of county seats). And even more ironically, as a member of the city council Cloud had introduced the resolution specifying the controversial charter revision after Judge Hickey had invalidated the city judiciary. Apparently Cloud's failure to win reelection to the council in early 1836 prompted him to shift his priorities dramatically.

Partisans on each side echoed the theme of city versus county. Charterites predicted catastrophe if Lexington lost her status as a municipal corporation. The county court would once again have a hand in administering town business and it would do so incompetently, its members already overburdened with other responsibilities and taxed with an inefficient organization. At a public meeting held shortly before the special election Daniel Mayes, a prominent Whig lawyer from Lexington, pointed to the hypocrisy of county court members who were denouncing the undemocratic city judiciary, but who themselves sat on a self-perpetuating tribunal. Mayes and others also emphasized that the county would once again tax city residents, should voters repeal the charter. City partisans also complained that loss of corporation status would make Lexington more dependent on the county's ineffective law enforcement.

Repealers countered that city officials operated the least effective and most repressive system of law enforcement. Although the city court handed out severe judgments compelling the convicted to pay exorbitant fines and court costs and to serve lengthy sentences in the city workhouse, the city police seldom solved more serious crimes. Charter opponents also submitted that the cost of city government climbed annually without attendant benefits. They clamored for a return to the good old days of less government and lower taxes.

Although they were unable to vote in the special election, county residents eagerly joined in the debate over the merits of the charter, mostly on the side of the repealers. Dependent upon Lexington as a market for their surplus timber, rural residents still resented the attempts of the city government to regulate the selling of wood. Asserting that most farmers were deeply offended by the "extravagances" of the amended city charter, one of the *Gazette*'s correspondents argued that repeal provided the only sure way to restore harmony between town and countryside. Another predicted that unless they were restrained by the voters, the city fathers would soon pass new ordinances encroaching upon the liberties of rural entrepreneurs and might even compel them to tip their hats to urban "aristocrats." Others expressed their agreement with these writers, contending that repeal would bring some humility back to the power-hungry corps of city officials.

Despite all of the oratory and printed invective, the repealers narrowly failed in their attempt to return Lexington to the status of an unincorporated town under the control of the county court. By a vote of 379 to 323 the city residents rejected the attempt to repeal. Undaunted, opponents of the city did not abandon their war on the revised charter. Citing the closeness of the vote, they maintained that the charterites must offer some concessions in order to placate the sizable minority that still resented city policy. Several Democratic candidates for the legislature pledged to continue the fight for repeal. In spite of their victory, charterites appeared conciliatory in the autumn of 1836, and shortly thereafter the new General Assembly revised the city charter in ways meeting most of the demands of the dissidents. The revision created a separate judge of the city court, restored the mayor to his position as chief executive of the city, and revived the ward system of representation on the city council. The ease with which the combatants achieved their compromise markedly contrasted with the intensity of their previous battles.

Fayette County and Lexington were not alone in their struggle over political supremacy within the local constitution. Jefferson County and Louisville confronted one another in a similar dispute in 1835. At issue in this episode was control of the public square. The county owned the buildings on the square but shared their occupation with the city. Because of the delapidated condition of these structures, new ones would have to be built, but the two governments disagreed over the method of financing the construction. The county argued that the city should share the cost of construction but not the ownership of the buildings. The city contended that either the county alone should pay for the construction or it should give the public square to the city, which would then pay for the new buildings and lease parts of them to the county. County officials rejected both proposals, labeling them inequitable and illegal.

Faced with county intransigence and bolstered by public displeasure over the run-down condition of the county-city buildings, city politicians launched a campaign for Louisville to secede from Jefferson County and become a separate county. They arranged to have the necessary legislation introduced into the General Assembly and began a public relations drive in Louisville newspapers. It soon became evident that the secession effort was being directed by Louisville Whigs who were increasingly frustrated by the Democratic domination of Jefferson County government. Complementing its campaign for a new county, the Whig newspaper, the *Louisville Journal,* blasted Worden Pope, accusing the prominent Democratic politician of controlling county government with the aid of his large family. So entrenched were the Popes, the *Journal* lamented sarcastically, that it was a shame the family was "not prolific enough to furnish a great lazy, lubberly boy for every office, not only in the . . . county, but throughout the state." The paper then gleefully noted that since most of the Popes resided in the city, they would have to move or compete with the rest of the city residents for places in the government of the new county.

County partisans publicly deplored the effort to create another county, arguing that taxes would soar in both Jefferson County and Louisville and that secession was unconstitutional. Privately, county officials hastily strove for a compromise, which was achieved after the two sides agreed to the appointment of a joint committee. The committee settled upon a formula to divide the expenses of construction, the public square remained county property, and the legislature allowed the Louisville County bill to lapse. Periodically throughout the remainder of the century Louisville and Jefferson County fought over the public square. In 1868, after negotiations failed, the county levied a tax against the city for a share of construction costs for a new jail. The city refused to pay the tax but finally came to terms with the county. Tensions between town and country sporadically flared up in Fayette County also, with geographical representation in county government arousing the most conflict. After the Civil War, county residents continually complained that the city controlled more and more of the county offices. But despite these complaints, Lexington continued its ascendancy in county government throughout most of the remainder of the century.

Although two of the commonwealth's most important counties experienced a good deal of conflict, relations between town and country were harmonious in most parts of the state. And in most communities the county remained supreme in the hearts and affairs of their inhabitants.

4

CONFLICT AND LAWLESSNESS

Whether in the form of vigilantism, feuds, riots, gangsterism, simple felony, or war, nineteenth-century Kentucky in many ways specialized in lawlessness and disorder. The Civil War disrupted many county governments and heightened an already festering crime problem. Reconstruction further intensified lawlessness and pitted many counties against the federal government when it attempted to encroach upon their control over local affairs.

Throughout the Civil War, Kentucky's commitment to the Union cause was at best tentative. Families, friends, churches, and political parties divided over the issue. In many respects, the county symbolized the commonwealth's dilemma and led her drift to organized chaos. Sheriffs in some counties collected taxes and turned them over to the pro-Confederate Provisional Government. In other counties sheriffs were intimidated by rebel guerrillas and found it impossible to collect taxes, enforce judgments, or carry out the simplest of responsibilities. Most sheriffs found it necessary at least to obtain special legislation permitting a certain leeway in the execution of official business. Not surprisingly, many sheriffs and other county officers resigned their offices in the face of torn loyalties and paramilitary harassment.

Within counties, officers sometimes came into conflict with one another in attempts to control county government. Early in the war, justices of the peace prevented the county judge of Wolfe County from holding court because he was suspected of Southern sympathies. In 1862, a loyal justice held court, purported to fire the sheriff and all others of rebel taint, and attempted to govern the county. Many doubted the legality of his actions, however, and the county languished for several months in a state of semianarchy.

War also disrupted county elections. In some counties disloyal sheriffs refused to hold elections, and private citizens had to assume control of the ballot box. In others federal troops intimidated voters, keeping all but the steadfast Union supporters from the polls. In some cases the legislature invalidated the results of coerced elections, but in most, Unionists won without challenge.

Peace did not end the turmoil in Kentucky, but in contrast to their performance in wartime, counties displayed rare unity with regard to federal policy. Because of the presence of large numbers of newly emancipated blacks, Congress voted to extend the jurisdiction of the Freedmen's Bureau to Kentucky. Designed to assist former slaves in their adjustment to freedom, the bureau soon encountered stiff opposition from county governments whose jurisdiction it most directly challenged. The bureau primarily oversaw the apprenticing and care of black orphans, indigents, and vagrants—traditional areas of concern for county courts. Undermanned, poorly budgeted, and highly unpopular, the bureau depended for its success on cooperation with the county courts.

The counties soon made it clear that such cooperation would not be forthcoming. Emboldened by a recently passed statute giving preference to former owners in the apprenticing of black children, the county courts bound out young blacks to their ex-masters in wholesale fashion.

Often they did this without consulting parents or nearest relatives of the children, in direct violation of the law. In many counties, judges bound out children to former masters who then hired them out to third parties in blatant violation of the provisions of their indentures. By mid-1867 it was apparent to most bureau officials that the county courts were perpetuating a kind of slavery in the guise of indentures of apprenticeship. One judge went so far as to declare the Freedmen's Bureau Act inapplicable to Kentucky, even though the statutory language clearly indicated otherwise.

Bureau officials intervened in some county court apprenticeship proceedings and occasionally succeeded in overturning illegal indentures and protecting the rights of blacks. But such cases amounted to a small fraction of the total. Efforts by the bureau to deal informally with county judges and other county officials likewise usually proved unavailing. So too did direct dealings with white masters of apprentices.

Their efforts at negotiation and compromise having failed, the bureau turned for advice to James Speed, a prominent Louisville attorney and former United States attorney general. After studying the state statute and county court practice, Speed advised the bureau to seek relief in the federal courts. While the federal courts inevitably overturned county court indentures issued in violation of the rights of freedmen, few petitions ever reached those tribunals. In short, the counties largely succeeded in frustrating the efforts of the bureau to ease the plight of black apprentices; simultaneously they created their own special brand of servitude.

The bureau enjoyed a little more success in its dealings with counties on the question of caring for indigent blacks. Shortly after the war's end, the legislature passed a special poll tax on blacks to fund their poor relief. Bureau officials complained that many counties failed to spend the tax for its intended purpose. These counties simply underwrote former slaveowners who wished to retain their slaves but could not afford to feed and house them. Despite bureau charges, the evidence suggests that some counties made at least partial efforts to provide poor blacks with minimal funds. But many others carried out the law in ways benefiting whites, paying scant attention to the needs of blacks.

County officials likewise utilized their jurisdiction over vagrants to continue slavery in Kentucky after the Thirteenth Amendment had been ratified. Empowered to arrest suspected vagrants and turn them over to circuit courts for trial, county officials eagerly snatched up suspicious-looking blacks by the droves. Circuit courts, too, proved especially willing to convict blacks of vagrancy and sell them into involuntary servitude for extended periods of time, the traditional nineteenth-century penalty for such offenders regardless of skin color.

The place of the counties in Kentucky's so-called Reconstruction clearly revealed their immense power in the nineteenth-century commonwealth. Not even the federal government could force them to give up traditional areas of local control. And, at the same time, the counties led white Kentucky's successful fight to preserve the antebellum social order.

Counties controlled crime far less successfully. Twentieth-century crime pales in comparison with the nineteenth-century criminal assault on the daily lives of Kentuckians (and Americans in general). In many ways the counties lay at the root of the problem. County officials remained the central figures of law enforcement throughout the century. Their general failure to carry out their responsibilities, and in some cases their willing participation in criminal acts, accounted in large part for the great crime wave of the period.

The presence of at least nine separate vigilante movements in Kentucky before 1850 attests to the prevalence of crime during the antebellum period. Usually not paramilitary in method or motivation, prewar criminals seldom committed felonies in the name of honor or patriotism; they simply robbed, maimed, and murdered for personal profit or vengeance. During and after the Civil War, the pure criminal was still abroad, but he was often joined in the field of pillage by brigands with a false sense of honor based on family, race, nation, or geographic section. Vigilantism, itself a form of lawlessness designed to stem lawlessness, naturally continued to flourish in such an atmosphere.

The Ku Klux Klan was the most spectacular form of paramilitary organization operating in the cause of misplaced patriotism. Derived from a variety of pro-Southern guerrilla movements of the war, the Klan flourished throughout the Reconstruction period in Kentucky. Even without a system of centralized control, local Klans attained much more power in Kentucky than in any other state outside the former Confederacy. Although the Democratic party always denied involvement and prominent party members and newspapers condemned the movement, the Klan devoted part of its activities to disrupting Republican meetings (especially if blacks were present) and intimidating would-be Republican voters (especially if they were black). The organization (or, more appropriately, organizations) also made it a practice to terrorize blacks generally, whether they were acting politically or not. In short, it was the special mission of the Klan to preserve the white man's Kentucky for the white man. But the Klan's criminal activities also sometimes took a more traditional form. Often a local Klan organization abandoned its patriotic cover and performed blatant acts of robbery, mayhem, and murder in order to line the pockets of its members or to gratify some bizarre notion of personal honor not associated with race or state. (Guerrilla bands had operated in much the same way during the war.)

By the very nature of their activity, Klans presented county officials with a problem of law enforcement—at least in theory. Since governors (all Democrats) refused to order the state guard to put down the Klan because in their opinion the problem was either local or nonexistent, it was up to county officials as the traditional officers of law enforcement to put the Klan out of business. No such result ever occurred. Those county officers who became actively involved with the Klan did so as members, not as antagonists. Disinterest rather than law enforcement stopped the Klan, if it was ever stopped.

By the late 1870s the Klan began to decline as an instrument of terror, but another sinister social institution soon took its place—the feud. Also in many ways born of the war and nurtured by its lingering antagonisms, feuds gripped many counties between 1875 and 1895, plunging some into conditions of anarchy. Not only did county officials fail to suppress these antisocial manifestations, but they often contributed to them. The counties as political institutions so entangled themselves in the post-war feuds that some Kentuckians advocated abolishing a few of them as a method of suppressing the violence.

Nowhere is the connection between county politics and feuds better illustrated than in the Rowan County turmoil of 1884–1887. In the summer of 1884, Republicans and Democrats engaged in a particularly intense campaign over the sheriffalty, resulting in the narrow victory of the Republican, Cook Humphrey. During an election night fight in a Morehead tavern, Floyd Tolliver, a prominent Democrat, wounded John Martin, an influential Republican, and another Democrat, Solomon Bradley, was killed. After several months of threat and counterthreat, Martin killed Tolliver, thereby provoking the wrath of the county's most powerful family. After arresting Martin for murder, Sheriff Humphrey placed his fellow Republican in the Montgomery County jail in order to protect him from the vengeance of the Tollivers. Not to be outmaneuvered, the Tollivers forged a court order for Martin's release to the Rowan County jail and spirited him onto a train bound for Morehead despite his protestations that he was about to be the victim of a frame-up. Martin's predictions came true; a gang of Tolliver sympathizers intercepted the train, dragged Martin from it, and murdered him.

Martin's murder sparked a two-and-one-half-year period of bloody conflicts involving families, political parties, and county officials. Early in 1885, the Martin gang ambushed and wounded Taylor Young, son of Democratic County Attorney Zachary Young. Retribution quickly followed as the Tollivers publicly vowed to drive Republican Sheriff Humphrey and his deputies out of the county or bury them within because they had allegedly conspired with John Martin to kill Floyd Tolliver and bushwacked Taylor Young. In April the two sides waged a pitched battle on the streets of Morehead forcing Humphrey into hiding and almost all of the other county officers into temporary retirement. In midsummer, the Tollivers located Humphrey in the house of John Martin's mother. They flushed out Humphrey (who somehow managed to escape, stopping only after he reached Kansas), killed two of his deputies, and apprehended two of the Martin daughters on fraudulent charges.

Maintaining the initiative, the Tollivers next trumped up charges that the absent Humphrey and his deputies had conspired to assassinate County Attorney Young; planning to use these charges as their own defense, they surrendered themselves for a preliminary hearing on the murder of Humphrey's deputies. In order to ensure themselves a partisan hearing, they forced the Republican county judge to disqualify himself, clearing the way for a friendly Democratic justice of the peace to sit with a Republican colleague as the examining court. In an unconvincing show of nonpartisanship, County Attorney Young withdrew from the case. (This was hardly the heroic act that he himself professed, since he had been the subject of the alleged Humphrey assassination conspiracy and remained an active participant in the raging feud.) Young and the rest of the Tolliver gang dropped any pretense of judicial restraint when Governor J.

Proctor Knott, growing increasingly disgusted with Rowan County's antics, sent in the attorney general as special prosecutor. Although the attorney general exposed the Humphrey conspiracy as a fabrication and the Tollivers offered no other plausible defense for their murderous actions, the Democratic justice of the peace voted to discharge them, thereby allowing the defendants to go free. To compound the travesty, the Tollivers next arranged for a packed grand jury to indict the elder Mrs. Martin for poisoning a turkey.

In the following year the Tollivers pursued their reign of terror with the same relish as before. In August they secured complete control of the county government by winning every one of the offices except that of county judge, which was appropriately filled by a cowardly Republican who could barely read and write. Completing the official tyranny, Craig Tolliver, head of the gang, secured election as police judge of Morehead in early 1887. In June of that year, the Tollivers turned once more to fraud and violence. They imprisoned a former ally, a certain Dr. Logan, for allegedly conspiring to assassinate County Attorney Young (the eternal victim) and then shot Logan's two sons in the back after promising them safe conduct to the county jail.

This latest outrage proved the undoing of the Tollivers. The surviving son, Boone Logan, after vainly appealing to Governor Knott for military intervention by the state guard, organized a vigilante group which on June 22, 1887, surprised the Tollivers, killing Craig Tolliver and several of his most powerful associates in the battle that ensued. The Tollivers continued their resistance, sending to another county for reinforcements. Faced with this new threat to civil order, Governor Knott at last sent in state troops. Although the military kept the peace, it could not prevent the county and commonwealth attorneys from conspiring with a packed grand jury to indict several of the regulators for murder. Fortunately for the vigilantes, the petit jury acquitted the defendants of all charges. So outrageous had the feud become in the public's eye that the normally conservative General Assembly only narrowly defeated a bill to abolish the rebellious county.

Other feuds stemmed from overzealous county politicking. The election for county judge in Breathitt County in 1878 revived antagonisms originating in the Civil War. Shortly after the election, County Judge J. W. Burnett led one of the factions in a pitched battle against the other in the streets of Jackson, the county seat. On the following day unknown persons ambushed and killed Burnett as he and his "gang of toughs" led a captured opponent to jail. Burnett's death only caused his survivors to fight the harder, with the sheriff leading the attack "as a partisan." Other county officers took leaves of absence or resigned. None of the justices of the peace would stand in for Burnett, and the circuit judge refused to hold court. Reluctantly, Governor James B. McCreary sent in state troops to restore order, however temporarily. Subsequent battles would prompt observers to refer to the county as "Bloody Breathitt."

Although it began because of the machinations of a disloyal business associate, Perry County's feud of 1887–1889 soon became entangled in county politics. Most county officials allied with the Eversole family, one of the principals in the fracas. Joe Eversole's father-in-law had been county judge and after August 1888 Eversole's brother took over the office. Neither would issue arrest warrants against members of the family. Sheriff James L. Howard displayed similar tendencies, refusing to arrest two notorious desperadoes because they were his "friends." Those relatives or friends of the family who somehow found themselves in jail usually escaped with the assistance of friendly Sheriff Howard. The grand jury, also heavily stacked with Eversoles, refused to return indictments. The Eversoles' sworn enemies, the French family and their friends, finding themselves largely locked out of county government, in self-defense hired a special "posse" of Breathitt County hoodlums. Once more the governor sent in troops, but as soon as they left, fighting resumed and the feud simmered throughout the remainder of the century.

Politics, family pride, racial tension, and ultimately a falling out among relatives contributed to the Garrard County feuds of 1874–1877. The maintenance of power within the county government was the overriding concern of the combatants. The Kennedy family remained at the center of the storm throughout its duration, the most prominent members being Ebbert (known to most as "Uncle Eb") and his nephew, Grove. Ebbert was the leader of the family and county boss of the Democratic party. He had held various offices of county government, including those of justice of the peace, surveyor, and county court clerk. As circuit court clerk and master commissioner in 1874, he administered many of the estates of the county, since most of the residents died without leaving wills. Eb's political prowess, his control over significant amounts of property, his powerful position in local government, and his leadership of a large and closely knit family made him the most influential citizen of the county. His most trusted and effective ally was his nephew, Grove, whose quick draw, violent temper, and hard drinking made him a fearsome creature to most of his neighbors.

In 1874, Uncle Eb sought reelection as circuit court clerk. The recent enfranchisement of blacks had so strengthened the Republican party that Eb labeled himself an "independent Democrat" in an effort to win support from uncommitted voters. Despite his attempts at nonpartisanship and his intense campaigning, Eb faced strong opposition from J. K. Faulkner, an ally of William Sellers, the most influential Republican in the county. Several weeks before election day, Eb grew desperate and made a deal with Sellers. Eb promised to throw some Democratic support to the Republican candidate for county clerk if Sellers would undercut Faulkner in the circuit court clerk's race. Despite assurances of Sellers's support, Eb lost the election and quickly concluded that he had been doublecrossed. Refusing to give up without a fight, Eb contested the election results and kept his office in the interim. Not content with these official procedures, he openly denounced Sellers, accusing him of a wide variety of cowardly acts.

Such verbal abuse eventually brought Eb to a confrontation with Sellers on the streets of Lancaster. As Sellers was about to discharge his pistol into Eb's face, Grove Kennedy, standing in a window above, ordered his withdrawal. Fearing a full-blown feud, certain citizens of the county telegraphed the commander of federal troops in Louisville to send a peace-keeping detachment to Lancaster. Exhibiting their contempt for such outside interference, Eb and a henchman, on the day following the arrival of the troops, stood in front of the courthouse and baited a group of pro-Sellers blacks with racial slurs. Soon afterwards the blacks appeared with late-model rifles. In the gun fight that followed, a member of the Kennedy clan was killed and the blacks were sent scurrying to Sellers's home, which they converted into an armed fortress. The next day the Sellers group wounded Squire Yeaky, a Kennedy ally, and attacked Eb Kennedy's home, wounding one of his grandchildren.

Securing numerous reinforcements, Eb and Grove Kennedy led an attack on Sellers's home, sending Sellers into exile from the county and his black allies into the public square where they finally surrendered after state troops arrived to reinforce the federal detachment. His political enemies either in surrender or hiding out, Uncle Eb once more seized the reins of county political power and began anew to administer intestate estates.

Ironically, Eb's final feud was with nephew Grove, who disputed his uncle's administration of his wife's estate. Unable to settle their differences judicially, Grove shot Eb dead in the courthouse in full view of the horrified local circuit judge. After being apprehended and then escaping, Grove eventually surrendered himself for trial. He was released after a jury was unable to agree on a verdict.

Rival families and their battles over county office also accounted for the Clay County feud of 1898–1901. Since before the Civil War members of the White and Garrard families feuded over politics and more trivial matters, such as hound dogs. In 1898, their fury attained new heights in a struggle over the sheriffalty. Whichever clan controlled this office often escaped apprehension and prosecution for crimes committed against the other. After a fierce struggle, the Whites (Democrats) retained control of the office despite the efforts of the Garrards (Republicans) to attract the support of dissident Democrats. Following the election, the clans squabbled over timber rights on adjoining properties and ultimately vented their frustrations in a series of murderous ambushes. State troops momentarily stilled the argument and held three of the offending Garrard clan for trial. Passions were renewed when the Whites assassinated one of the three as he stood near the opening of his militia tent. Governor W. O. Bradley conducted special meetings on the problem to no avail, and it took the patient negotiations of a courageous circuit court judge three years later to end the raging feud. The disputants signed a formal peace treaty on March 13, 1901.

There can be no doubt but that the county figured prominently in the feuds of nineteenth-century Kentucky. Not only county politics and negligent county peace officers, but the large number of counties contributed to the local wars. "These little county organisms are storm centers from which feuds are created . . . from which antagonisms radiate," argued a delegate to the Constitutional Convention of 1890–1891. As he saw it, many feuds began over the spoils of county office and perpetuated themselves amidst the natural hostilities of closely knit communities. Elaborating upon this theme, the *Courier-Journal* charged that a "county brawl" inevitably involved large segments of a typically small county, and thus it was impossible to find impartial peace officers or juries. In addition, the smallness of most counties contributed to tensions. In a population closeted together within confined geographical boundaries, familiar with one another's weaknesses and ambitions, competing against one another for political and economic leverage, it was almost certain that normal tensions would produce abnormal reactions. These conditions, united with gnawing poverty, illiteracy, lack of such stable institutions as churches, and lingering frustrations from the war, produced Kentucky's feuds and high crime rate.

Feuds, of course, were only the most sensational form of lawlessness. Ordinary crime also mushroomed in the second half of the century, drawing loud complaints from politicians and citizens alike that peace officers stood by while thugs robbed, maimed, and murdered. The *New York Times* reported that Kentucky trailed the nation in law enforcement. Governors constantly carped at county officials for failing to enforce the laws. Yet the problem was not simply one of electing more resolute men. Despite the presence of large numbers of cowardly or criminal county officers, other conditions contributed to the crime wave.

The most important officer in the state's corps of law enforcers, the sheriff, found himself burdened with so many other tasks that he often had little time to apprehend criminals. Tax collecting alone took an inordinate amount of time. Also the fees the sheriff received for his civil responsibilities far exceeded any he could collect from crime-fighting efforts. Nor did the sheriff possess adequate instruments with which to cope with much of the state's crime. Even his critics admitted that the posse comitatus, composed of those volunteers whom the sheriff could persuade to lend a hand at a moment's notice, afforded little relief against organized bands of criminals. By the time the sheriff had convinced enough civilians that they should risk their lives to protect the community, the outlaws had usually secured themselves in hiding.

Even those few sheriffs who took their law enforcement duties seriously sometimes found themselves in the thick of feuds and other outrages. A typical example was Walter Saunders, who retired in 1876 after a highly successful career as sheriff of Lincoln County. Within the county, Saunders performed effectively and honestly, apprehending all types of criminals from corn rustlers to such highwaymen as the notorious Jim Bridgewater. But outside the county, he descended to the level of a common criminal (for example, he joined Eb Kennedy in his gun battle with William Sellers for control of Garrard County). After his retirement from the sheriffalty, Saunders became embroiled in a feud with Jim Berthuram, whose brother he had killed while arresting a gang of thieves. In early 1878, Saunders made a citizen's arrest of another of Berthuram's brothers and two friends who were accused of robbing and torturing an elderly couple and participating in a general wave of crime encompassing Lincoln, Rockcastle, and Garrard counties. After driving Jim Berthuram into hiding, Saunders took his three captives to the Rockcastle County jail. Not content with this bit of heroics, he subsequently led a party of nearly a hundred men to the jail, dragged the trio to a nearby tree, and promptly lynched them. Appropriately, Saunders met his end in the same year, when he unsuccessfully stormed Richmond in an effort to avenge his brother who had been beaten by the town marshal. To complete the paradox, his widow discovered herself penniless—her husband had exhausted the family estate bailing out debtors against whom he had executed judgments while serving as sheriff.

Governors commanded the most effective weapon against collective lawlessness—the state guard. But it was impossible to send troops to every county where crime raged uncontested, and after the soldiers left, criminal activities usually were as prevalent as ever. Moreover, governors tended to resist calls for troops; crime fighting was essentially a local problem, they said, and use of the state guard was too expensive a measure.

Governors contributed to crime not only through inaction, but through the too liberal use of their pardoning power. According to the *New York Times*, which kept a fascinated watch on Kentucky throughout the second half of the century, the "reckless exercise of the pardoning power by the Governor has been a direct incitement to crime." But one of those most often accused of leniency, Governor Luke P. Blackburn, contended that he granted pardons only because of his humanitarian instincts. Appalled by conditions at the state penitentiary where prisoners were stuffed into four-by-six-foot cells and died at "a fearful rate," Blackburn believed it his duty to free as many as possible. Blackburn also contended that many of the prisoners had committed only trivial crimes and had been charged by prosecuting attorneys eager to bolster their incomes through fees earned by trying cases.

And it was true that prosecutors contributed to the crime problem by obtaining convictions of petty criminals while failing in their efforts against major ones. Often either young and inexperienced or old and incompetent, county and commonwealth attorneys usually found themselves completely overshadowed by defense counsel. So scandalous was the situation that wealthy families with criminal victims normally hired private counsel to assist in the prosecution of the offender.

Judges, juries and legislators likewise added to the burden. Judges often failed to keep their dockets current, refused to try cases in feud-torn counties, and displayed undue leniency toward hardened criminals. Frequently composed of deadbeats who hung around courthouses hoping to earn a quick fee, juries acted no more resolutely. A Nicholas County murderer, sentenced by a jury in 1877 to only eleven years in prison, thanked the twelve men, admitting that he believed "he deserved the extreme penalty of the law" and expressing surprise at the light sentence. Critics charged that legislatures were dominated by criminal lawyers who wished to bolster their own professional advantage by composing a lax criminal code.

County officials as well as criminals profited from crime, since the state was required by statute to pay most of the cost of enforcing the criminal law. Annual outlays for this purpose steadily increased throughout the century so that by 1870 a sizable portion of the state budget went to crime fighting. Unscrupulous county peace officers added to the expense by setting up collusive crimes and fraudulent claims. It was not unusual for a sheriff, jailer, or constable to arrange a friendly fight between two cronies, one of whom would be slightly wounded. After the other "escaped" to an appointed spot in another county, the peace officers would give chase, apprehend the "criminal," and transport him back to the local jail. For this and for escorting him to circuit court (where he would be acquitted), the officers would receive fees from the commonwealth.

Complain though they might, Kentuckians did little in the nineteenth century to cure the problem of increasing crime and inadequate law enforcement. Citizens constantly petitioned the legislature for remedial action, but largely to no avail. Some turned to protest meetings; others resorted to vigilantism, and while this form of regulation produced temporary benefits in some counties, it normally became itself a sinister type of lawlessness. The best solution, never in the nineteenth century advanced beyond the planning stage, was the creation of a professional, specialized county police force.

Urban counties entertained the notion of county police departments during the last three decades of the nineteenth century. Jefferson County secured various laws from the General Assembly permitting the appointment of policemen, but only took advantage of the option for special events such as county fairs and horse races (and then at the expense of the proprietors requesting the protection). In 1876 a group of Fayette County residents petitioned the county court for the creation of a "county detective force" to render their "houses and property . . . more secure than they have been for a number of years." Even though the petitioners would have accepted a tax increase, believing that a reduction in crime would result in a net saving, the court refused to establish a detective force, expressing fears that it would evolve into a "secret police." County residents, citing the ease with which burglars robbed their houses, persisted in their demands for more adequate police protection, and in 1878 the legislature passed a statute permitting the county judge to appoint a constabulary of up to five men. Once more the court refused to act. Eight years later the legislature passed a broader law authorizing the counties of Fayette, Kenton, and Campbell to create police districts for designated suburban areas if taxpayers owning a majority of the assessed land so petitioned their county courts. Apparently more concerned with their tax rates than their security, taxpayers did not petition the courts in sufficient numbers, and no police departments were established. Kentuckians responded to crime as they did to bad roads; they constantly complained, but were unwilling to pay for solutions.

5

LITTLE ENGINES
OF IMPROVEMENT

IN AN AGE WHEN travel was difficult and sometimes impossible, it is not surprising that a major preoccupation of nineteenth-century Kentuckians was finding ways to improve transportation. Counties played an increasingly instrumental part in the search for and development of these schemes, whether involving paths and dirt roads or ferries, over which counties had specific jurisdiction, or turnpikes and railroads, over which they exercised increasing financial influence.

Dirt roads and macadamized turnpikes were Kentucky's primary avenues of transportation until after 1850, when railroads took on increasing importance. Most road-building projects were joint ventures, combining the resources of government with those of private enterprise. Turnpike companies built many of the major roads. Specially chartered by the legislature, they derived most of their capital from state and local government, the counties being the most important local source. Turnpikes offered the advantage of macadamized surfaces, which withstood the pressures of time and travel more readily than dirt roads. Unfortunately for the traveler, most of the roads constructed in the nineteenth century were of the latter type, the majority of them simply two dirt ruts. For many months of the year, rain and snow converted the ruts into muddy canals, rendering them impassable. Heavy rains washed some roads away, necessitating the building of new ones when dry weather finally appeared.

Counties maintained most of the free roads and some of the turnpikes, if the companies that had built them no longer had the funds to service them. Throughout the nineteenth century the labor tax remained the principal method by which counties furnished manpower to repair roads. Originally every able-bodied man in the county owed as many days' work on the local road as the road overseer directed, although eventually the legislature limited each man's workload to a specific number of days. The county court appointed road overseers or surveyors to supervise the labor; usually there were at least fifty of these officials in each county. Wealthier landowners normally hired substitutes rather than work roads themselves, and later in the century they simply paid a certain sum in lieu of work. But the average farmer could not afford to pay proxies and was subject to "road calls" at any moment.

Needless to say, the labor tax was not a popular institution in nineteenth-century Kentucky. During harvest the road calls brought forth especially loud cries of protest, although the service was never at any time gladly given. In the early part of the century, whites so complained at having to work alongside blacks that the General Assembly prohibited slaveowners from sending slaves in their stead. Conscientious road overseers earned only scorn from their neighbors, who bitterly resented having to leave their fields to fill in chuckholes and rebuild roads. It was not uncommon for farmers to flee their houses and hide in the nearest woods rather than be served work summonses. In such an atmosphere it was perhaps inevitable that most overseers worked the roads only those few days necessary to avoid prosecution. Consequently most roads remained primitive paths, suitable for passage in only the most favorable weather.

Naturally many Kentuckians despaired over the generally deplorable condition of their roads and the system by which most were maintained, and some advocated specific reforms. In 1830 at the prompting of Robert Wickliffe, Sr., himself a state senator and one of the wealthiest men in Fayette County, the legislature enacted statutes permitting counties to alter the old road system. If it accepted the change, a county would substitute for the labor tax a per capita money tax, which would be used to pay road commissioners and laborers. Most counties that considered reform put the question to the voters, but only a few ever secured majorities for the adoption of the new system. Some of these subsequently repealed the new ordinances, apparently finding money taxes even more unpleasant than road labor.

While agreeing to an optional reform for the rest of the counties, Wickliffe insisted upon a mandatory revision for Fayette. Salaried commissioners and paid laborers would replace overseers and self-help, and the results would be, in Wickliffe's opinion, revolutionary. Fayette County would soon be blessed with the best roads in the commonwealth, her economy would soar to even greater heights of prosperity, and the general public would no longer be saddled with the onerous labor tax. But Wickliffe's prognostications proved overoptimistic. The county court, unhappy at having to relinquish part of its jurisdiction to a new group of public officials, succeeded in delaying implementation of the road law. When finally the court authorized the election of road commissioners, most voters staged their own protest by refusing to vote for any of the candidates for the new positions. A few did vote, but those commissioners who were theoretically "elected" came to the next session of the county court and resigned their positions. A disappointed Wickliffe secured repeal of the reform legislation at the next session of the General Assembly.

Even turnpikes failed to afford their chief promotors the success they had confidently forecast. The economy of counties in which the macadamized roads were built hardly ever attained the levels predicted by turnpike builders, and the roads themselves often deteriorated because of inadequate maintenance. By the end of the Civil War it was evident to many that in some counties turnpikes were actually impediments to economic growth. Critics in Fayette and surrounding counties complained that high tolls kept farmers away from Lexington. These observers also noted that many tollkeepers behaved rudely to customers, allowed friends and relatives to pass without charge, and failed to guarantee the safe and secure passage of clients. Sagging revenues contributed to the growing disillusionment of investors. By 1880, serious movements to convert turnpikes to free roads under the supervision of the counties themselves had commenced in many places. In 1890 Fayette County became one of the first to endorse this reform, and many other counties followed suit in the next decade. Such change did not occur without great controversy and some bloodshed, however, as witness the turnpike riots throughout Kentucky in the 1890s and early twentieth century.

Counties exerted influence over other forms of transportation in nineteenth-century Kentucky. During the antebellum period, especially, their ability to grant franchises to ferry operators and to regulate their rates proved very significant in an age of relatively few bridges. Ferry operators along the Ohio River had especially lucrative enterprises, and applicants often waged spirited battles for the exclusive right to operate a franchise in a particular area. The prominent Taylor family of Campbell County contested the city of Newport's ferry rights for more than twenty years. Maysville successfully resisted the efforts of four of her private citizens to compete with her ferry service to Ohio, and Covington likewise prevailed against a would-be private competitor.

In 1830, Kentuckians began their love-hate affair with the railroad, the magnificent innovation that was supposed to bring them so much happiness but often brought only grief. From 1830 to 1850, railroad promoters in the commonwealth were noted more for false starts than for successes. And in the process of their failures, railroad men sometimes raided county treasuries. Fayette County's abortive relationship with the Louisville, Cincinnati, and Charleston Railroad from 1836 to 1840 illustrates some of the frustrations attending early county investment.

Striving to connect the Ohio Valley with the Carolina coast, backers of the Louisville, Cincinnati, and Charleston Railroad predicted that the construction of their line would bring new markets and wealth to central Kentucky. Business and government leaders of Fayette County were anxious to revitalize the county's economy (which had been losing ground to Jefferson County's since the introduction of the steamboat), and for this reason they urged the governments of the county and Lexington to purchase large chunks of the company's stock on the condition that the line would terminate at Lexington rather than at Louisville. Representatives of the railroad willingly secured an amendment to the company's charter providing that Lexington would be the railroad's Kentucky terminus and further promised that construction would begin there. In December 1836 the Fayette County Court voted to subscribe to $100,000 worth of railroad stock to be financed by a special ad valorem tax on real property.

Many in the county expressed little joy about the proposed stock subscription. By late March 1837 the *Kentucky Gazette*, itself a promoter of the venture, reported that many residents of the county opposed the investment. Soon thereafter, organized opposition to the subscription manifested itself in the form of meetings held in various parts of the county. Dissidents who opposed the railroad venture demanded that the county court hold a special election on the subscription and be bound by its results. The railroad supporters made valiant efforts to rally support, holding meetings of their own and bombarding the newspapers with letters, but the county court deemed unrest over the investment to be so profound that it reluctantly ordered a referendum on the question.

The announcement of a special election touched off an extended debate on the legality of the subscription and the merits of the railroad. Detractors said that it was unconstitutional for a county to invest in a private railroad and further predicted collapse of the venture. Proponents argued that the future welfare of the county's economy depended on rail routes to the East Coast and denounced opponents for trying to achieve tax savings at the expense of progress. In August, the voters of Fayette County approved the subscription by a margin of more than two to one, with county residents barely endorsing the measure in contrast to Lexington's overwhelming support.

The election victory proved to be the high point for the railroad and its supporters. Pledges of support were not forthcoming from other public sectors, and private investors could not take up the slack. By spring of 1838 the picture appeared so bleak that some in Fayette County advocated forfeiture of the subscription. Eschewing such drastic action, the county court voted to postpone collection of the annual installment until the railroad could furnish better proof of its solvency and intention to commence construction within the near future. The dreary condition of the company made such declarations impossible, and in November citizens of the county held a public meeting to anguish over their apparent loss. By spring of the following year the county court groped for ways to recoup its losses and voted to place surplus railroad funds in a special account for improvement of the county clerk's office. During the next three years the court made unsuccessful attempts to recover all or part of the $10,000 it had paid to the company, which had ceased operations in Kentucky without ever laying a single section of track in the commonwealth.

If Fayette County learned anything from its unhappy experience with the Louisville, Cincinnati, and Charleston Railroad, it was only a very temporary lesson. By 1851, it began to join other counties in considering investments in new railroad ventures. Such considerations marked the beginning of more than forty years of intimate county involvement with railroad schemes. At the same time the state government, which had invested more than $5,000,000 in turnpikes between 1812 and 1850, virtually bowed out of the transportation business for the rest of the century. Private funds continued to be scarce, and although towns and cities also invested heavily, counties were the major source of railroad capital in Kentucky during the last half of the nineteenth century. Unfortunately, for the counties, while this distinction once more highlighted their significance in the lives of nineteenth-century Kentuckians, it did not signal a departure from their record of poor financial planning. Counties seldom derived any profit from their railroad investments and often lost everything.

Before promoters of railroad ventures within county governments could begin their binge of investment, they first had to surmount certain constitutional objections to government assistance to private business. In 1851, more than 150 taxpayers of Mason County sought to prevent the county court from investing heavily in the Maysville and Lexington Railroad Company on the grounds that such involvement violated the state constitution. Despite extended arguments of counsel to the contrary and a lengthy, well-reasoned dissenting opinion by one justice, a majority on the Court of Appeals sustained the county's investment, thereby scotching for forty years serious legal arguments over the question. From that time on, critics of government aid to railroads in Kentucky stressed economic rather than constitutional problems.

Having surmounted the most serious legal challenge to their ventures, railroad promoters were free to unleash their highly organized and alluring campaigns to entice counties into subscribing huge amounts to their ventures. Such promotions often resembled carnivals and included flamboyant speeches, personal endorsements by political and military heroes, mass meetings evincing almost hysterical support, and predictions of perpetual prosperity. Woe to the county, the railroad men inevitably cautioned, that failed to join the national rush to railroads. Grass would soon grow in the streets of the county seat, farmland would decline in value, and commercial relations with other counties and states would deteriorate if the county refused to invest. The entrepreneurs who were puffing railroads invariably pointed to the supposed progress of neighboring counties as further inducement for participation. Counties with railroads would surely outdistance those without them.

Such oratory contributed to conflicts between counties over the location of proposed railroads and encouraged outside intervention in subscription battles. As Fayette County and Lexington continued the battle to regain their former position in the commonwealth's economy, Jefferson County and Louisville sought to undermine efforts to make Lexington a railroad hub. In 1851, Lexington newspapers reported that Louisvillians were encouraging "disaffected persons" in Boyle County to oppose a possible railroad route to Lexington in favor of one to Frankfort. Three years later Louisville sought ways to discourage the construction of the proposed Nashville and Cincinnati Railroad for fear that Lexington would become the southern focal point of a vast northern system of railroads. After the Civil War, the Louisville and Nashville Railroad, with headquarters in the county seat of Jefferson County and by far the most successful railroad of the commonwealth, strove to maintain its supremacy by stalling legislative approval of the Cincinnati Southern, which threatened to benefit Fayette County, and worked to frustrate other ventures which might work to the advantage of central Kentucky counties. In 1885, L & N agents are said to have appeared in Harrodsburg with plenty of "boodle" in order to scotch Mercer County's flirtation with the rival Louisville and Southern Railroad.

Other counties played similar games. Fayette County reportedly helped secure the defeat of Bourbon County's proposed subscription to the Paris and Maysville Railroad in 1870. In 1851, Boyle countians opposed routing of the Lexington and Danville Railroad through Harrodsburg because this might help the Harrodsburg economy at the expense of Danville. Almost simultaneously, a Franklin County delegation attempted to persuade Mercer County to build a railroad to Frankfort rather than to Lexington, while in 1872, Clark countians campaigned to have the Frankfort, Paris, and Big Sandy Railroad built through Mount Sterling rather than Owingsville. In 1869, Cincinnati's planned railroad south elicited delegations from several Kentucky counties attempting to influence the line's location, with Lexingtonians pledging money if the route ran through their city.

The railroad subscriptions also produced conflict between town and countryside. Although legislatures freely authorized counties to subscribe to railroad stock, they always required them first to secure voter approval. Cities and towns solidly approved such ventures for the most part, while rural residents normally opposed them. Town dwellers did not curtail their support even in the face of double taxation as residents of two separate local governments. Deeply resentful of being bound to taxes by urban majorities, rural residents began to demand that voters residing outside of county seats be required to endorse subscriptions separately before they became valid. One of the liveliest of the battles occurred in Bourbon County following the Civil War. Despite numerous petitions and personal appearances by promoters, the members of the Bourbon County Court refused to submit to the voters the question of a subscription to the stock of the Frankfort, Paris, and Big Sandy Railroad. Political leaders of Paris protested the court's intransigence, noting that the three justices of the peace who supported submission were all from Paris and represented more voters than the other eleven magistrates combined. All pleas to the court having failed, representatives from the railroad and Paris secured an amendment to the statute creating the company's charter. Under this amendment the county was compelled to hold an election on the subject of subscription.

Rural residents resented this latest ploy and denounced it as an attempt to usurp the duly constituted authority of the county court. Railroad supporters countered with the argument that the court had unlawfully prevented the voters from expressing themselves on the question of the subscription. "Rubbish!" cried the opponents, who lambasted the notion that a tyrannical majority could force a minority to pay taxes for projects it opposed. So the battle raged until election day, when voters narrowly endorsed the venture. After all this turmoil, the county never spent a penny on the road, for its backers failed to secure needed support from surrounding counties and private investors, and the scheme collapsed before Bourbon officials were to pay their first installment.

Bourbon County was not alone in experiencing controversy over a proposed railroad subscription. Virtually all such ventures encountered some opposition, and the predictions of dire consequences usually proved accurate. Many of the promised railroads were never built, and those that were often went through at least one reorganization that wiped out the counties' investments. In the spring of 1851, after much debate on the issue,

Fayette countians voted to invest $600,000 in the stock of three railroads. Other counties quickly followed suit, but none realized any permanent ownership in the concerns even though the roads were eventually built. Inaccurate cost estimates, unexpected geographical impediments, and lack of capital forced each road into bankruptcy, causing all of the counties to lose their investments entirely.

More protracted and equally frustrating were efforts of certain central Kentucky counties to underwrite a railroad connecting their region with the mineral-rich counties of eastern Kentucky. Known by various names and sometimes involving more than one company, the "Big Sandy" enterprise began in the 1850s and lasted well beyond the Civil War. Buoyed by promises of great wealth and expanded markets, the counties of Fayette, Greenup, Bath, Clark, and Montgomery and the city of Lexington subscribed in 1853 to over a million dollars of stock in the Lexington and Big Sandy Railroad Company. Underfinanced and overmanipulated, this line died in foreclosure shortly before the war. The dream of an eastern connection would not die, however, and a new Big Sandy company appeared in 1869, full of new hopes and financial needs.

With short memories and heady aspirations, Fayette, Montgomery, and Clark counties once more subscribed heavily to the endeavor but other county shareholders in the earlier venture refused to risk still more capital. By 1873 it was evident that the skeptics had been right again, as a group of New York speculators, led by the shrewd Collis P. Huntington, bought the Big Sandy for a small fraction of its subscribed value. Contending that they had been hoodwinked out of their investment, the county shareholders took the controversy to court and to the legislature, securing in the General Assembly a statute requiring a majority of the Big Sandy's directors to reside in Kentucky. Never one to run from a fight, Huntington attempted to buy up large numbers of the certificates entitling taxpayers—as investors—to shares of stock. The battle lasted until the two sides finally compromised in 1879, the counties forsaking their bid to retain substantial control and Huntington promising to complete the line within three years. Huntington kept his word, but as of July 1890 the Big Sandy had paid no dividends to its county investors.

Naturally the numerous railroad bankruptcies aroused deep feelings of hostility within those counties that had subscribed to the stock of the failures. This anger intensified when county taxpayers realized that their governments remained liable on bonds issued to pay for railroad stock. Believing they had been victimized by fraudulent eastern slicksters, many counties refused to continue paying interest on their bonds. In the face of this repudiation, bondholders often took their cases to court and inevitably secured judgments in their own favor, since they themselves were seldom parties to fraud. Faced with adverse judgments, counties generally assessed taxes to pay off liabilities on their bonds but found it impossible to collect the special levies from rebellious taxpayers. Possessed of judgments they could not enforce, bondholders usually had to agree to payment at a greatly reduced figure. Sometimes bondholder battles lasted for decades, as illustrated by an episode in Muhlenberg County.

In 1868, Muhlenberg County subscribed to $400,000 worth of stock in the Elizabethtown and Paducah Railroad, a venture touted by promoters as a sure way for the county to enhance its commerce and prosperity. Although it laid some track, the company did not survive the depression of 1873 and underwent reorganization, wiping out the county's stock interest. Because the company had neglected to deliver its stock certificates to the county in 1868, many within the county, ignorant of the law's technicalities, believed they had been cheated out of their investment. In 1874, outraged residents organized an Independent Order of Taxpayers and elected a county judge committed to repudiation. Predictably the judge and court of claims voted to stop paying interest on the bonds, precipitating a twenty-five-year fight between the county and its bondholders.

Experiencing temporary second thoughts about its defiance, the Muhlenberg County Court in 1878 secured special legislation from the General Assembly authorizing the county to establish a funding board empowered to compromise the railroad debt. But the board accomplished little. It met for several years before it could even agree on a system by which to compromise the debt, finally dissolving after voters refused to participate in the annual election of its members. Eventually the county issued some bonds in supposed settlement of the debt—but then repudiated them. Faced with this new recalcitrance, many bondholders obtained judgments from state and federal courts. By 1896, as the result of the judgments, the county tax levy had soared to over twelve dollars per $100 of valuation. But most of the tax was never collected, because the court-appointed collectors either refused to serve or were run out of the county by irate residents. The United States Supreme Court solidified the impasse by refusing to appoint a special collector under the supervision of the federal judiciary.

One bondholder who made his living by investing in repudiated bonds would not be frustrated by the stalemate. Organizing his own private army, he forced the county court to appoint him collector of the tax and then at gunpoint persuaded the taxpayers to pay. But most bondholders displayed no such brashness and did not receive a penny on their bonds until early in the twentieth century, when the dispute was finally settled by a more responsible county court. In the meantime, the county's economy stagnated under the cloud of its government's battered credit and near insolvency.

In other counties citizens resorted to more violent means to resolve their problems with bondholders. After failing to halt construction of the railroad by means of armed attacks, Marion County vigilantes attempted to prevent the sheriff from collecting the railroad tax. Green County residents burned down the barn of the railroad tax collector and threatened his deputies with the same treatment. Plunging the county into "a frightful state of disorder and anarchy," the tax resisters succeeded in their attempts to curtail county tax collection. Tongue in cheek, Taylor County offered to settle its indebtedness by giving bondholders its worthless railroad stock. Only a last-minute decision by the United States Supreme Court saved members of the Allen County Court from contempt-of-court jail sentences for failure to enforce judgments on repudiated bonds. Other counties resisted just as fiercely, some carrying their fights into the twentieth century.

6

FINANCES AND REFORM

No SUBJECT EXCITED nineteenth-century Kentuckians more than taxes, and no division of government played a greater part in taxation than the counties. County officials assessed and collected state and county taxes and spent county revenues. All phases of this system were controversial and, in some counties, outrageous.

A poll tax of up to three dollars per adult male constituted the principal county tax throughout the nineteenth century. Its defenders praised it as the only effective way to force the propertyless to contribute to the expenses of government. Its detractors damned it as "oppressive," "retrogressive," and a "product of a barbarous age." As the century passed, more and more states (mostly northern) abolished the tax so that by 1870 critics could declare the tribute "unworthy of a civilized nation in the nineteenth century."

In theory the poll tax may have been an excellent way to compel the poor to pay their fair share of the cost of government, but in practice it generally failed. Most evaded the tax by simply refusing to pay it, pleading no funds. Delinquency rates in most counties exceeded 20 percent of the eligible taxpayers. Some secured exemptions from the county court; others ignored the entire process, usually with impunity. On the other side of the economic spectrum, wealthy taxpayers welcomed the tax as a way to avoid the much greater burdens associated with ad valorem property taxes, although the latter type of tax was frequently levied to pay for such special projects as railroad subscriptions. Some wealthy residents escaped the poll tax entirely by securing the exemption normally granted the "aged."

Theoretically fairer, since it was based on the value of each taxpayer's personal and real property, in fact state taxation also contained many inequities. Because each taxpayer did his own evaluating, the assessor lacking the time and personnel to do it himself (and often the fortitude and competence), many succeeded in undervaluing their taxable property, and not a few withheld from assessment large chunks of land and personal belongings. The rich evaded and undervalued most successfully. In 1883, Governor Knott contended that Boyd County horses were assessed at a higher valuation than much finer steeds in Bourbon County, and two years later he noted that Indiana's assessed valuation was twice that of Kentucky's even though Kentucky had a greater taxable acreage.

Such inconsistencies and evasions not surprisingly sparked taxpayer revolts, the most sensational of which occurred in Pendleton County during the period from 1877 to 1879. There the county court taxed and borrowed at record levels, failing to account for expenditures, and sheriffs specialized in double taxation for some and none for others. Outraged taxpayers formed a committee of safety at a mass meeting early in 1877. After interviewing county officials and taxpayers, the committee accused the local government of discrimination against the poor, of misappropriation of public funds, and of failure to collect over $25,000 in delinquent back taxes. Although the county court rolled back the amount of the poll tax, it refused to publish a detailed accounting of expenditures or to change its procedures in the ways demanded by the reformers.

Frustrated by the intransigence of county officials, the

committee turned to the commonwealth attorney and grand jury for assistance. The jury investigated the problem and found that many of the committee's accusations rang true. But strangely it failed to produce indictments, referring the controversy back to the county court—which continued to resist meaningful reform. Over the next two years accusations and insults were traded back and forth, each side charging the other with corruption and immorality. Finally, the county began printing more detailed financial statements, making a better effort to collect back taxes, and collecting current taxes more uniformly. While the committee asserted that more revisions were in order, by 1879 taxpayer interest in the controversy abated and the impulse for further change withered and died.

County appropriation policy was no more satisfactory than the taxation system. Those with claims against the county had to submit them to the county court, wait for the court to approve them, and then wait still longer for the sheriff to collect enough taxes to pay them. This process sometimes took a year or longer, since the court seldom met more than twice a year on the business of its debts and sheriffs normally found it difficult to collect taxes rapidly and efficiently. Thus many who were dependent upon the government for their livelihood were forced to sell their claims against the county to professional brokers at reduced rates.

Adding to the burden of those doing business with counties or hired by them to perform specific services was the often inequitable method by which county officials processed claims. Although the county attorney was required by statute to screen all claims, he seldom did this effectively, and the members of the county court had to sift through the bills for themselves. Rather than spend the time to determine the validity of each claim, the courts often arbitrarily halved claims. Shrewd claimants, anticipating this, normally doubled the amount of their claims and suffered no loss. But more innocent creditors, not understanding the system or fearful of engaging in fraudulent practices, found themselves cheated out of half of their claims.

The method of paying county officials compounded the grievances of nineteenth-century Kentuckians. Fees rather than salaries accounted for the bulk of the income of most county officers. Only the county judge and county attorney received salaries, and in both cases the salaries were supplemented by fees for certain services. Since the amount of income received by officers depended upon the number of services they performed for county residents, needless or repetitious functions were encouraged. Even fee gouging could not raise the incomes of the officers of poorer counties to levels of respectability, but it did enable those of wealthier, more populous counties to achieve sizable incomes. The officers of Jefferson County sometimes earned as much as $40,000 annually, an income that attracted hordes of aspirants to these positions. Observers noted that no other class of citizens in the commonwealth "received better pay and did less work."

Typically the legislature responded slowly and inadequately to these grievances. It required certain counties to validate their claims more expeditiously and fairly but did almost nothing to insure their swifter liquidation. Toward the end of the century a few counties opted for a commission form of government, replacing the justices of the peace on the court of claims with three elected commissioners. Supporters argued that three businessmen could handle the financial burdens of the county much more efficiently than ten or twenty justices of the peace who hardly ever seemed to have much business acumen. Despite the reported success of this experiment, constitutional reformers did not make the change mandatory for all counties. Demands for the abolition of the fee system produced no results.

The failure of the General Assembly to respond satisfactorily to the fiscal shortcomings of Kentucky's counties stemmed from its own institutional deficiencies. The commonwealth's legislators were much more adept at presiding over the pageantry of politicking (burgoos, barbecues, and court day speeches), than they were at legislating. An observer contended that Kentucky's statutes were the laughingstock of the nation. So disarranged and illogical were the laws that one of them required commonwealth attorneys to enforce the criminal statutes, while another forbade them to practice law except in civil proceedings.

Stupidity, inattention, and laziness alone did not account for the sins of the legislature. That body also found itself increasingly bogged down in the mire of local and special legislation, a problem directly related to the fact that the counties were so numerous. Often legislatures responded to the needs of citizens and special interests on an individual basis rather than enacting general laws applicable to everyone. Thus, instead of formulating a general incorporation law that would establish standards for all would-be corporations and delegate their supervision to a separate administrative agency such as a bureau of corporations, the legislature itself chartered each company, taking the time to enumerate powers and limitations. In the same way, the legislature addressed itself to the problems of individual counties, granting this sheriff an extension of time in which to collect taxes and ratifying that county court's delinquent tax levy. By 1850, the General Assembly devoted most of its sessions to such local and special laws and spent almost no time on the general problems of the commonwealth, which, ironically, grew more acute as technology bound Kentuckians more closely together. The great number of requests for special legislation meant the assembly, which met only biennially after 1850, lacked sufficient time to consider each one adequately. It also meant that counties themselves largely controlled the legislation affecting their interests.

Normally when a county desired legislation its officers drafted a bill themselves or in conjunction with the local state representative and senator. Because of the tradition of legislative courtesy by which legislators did not challenge the bills of other legislators affecting their own local affairs, and because of the multitude of such proposals, the assembly did not have time to review local legislative bills with the care they demanded. Consequently counties actually possessed powers of legislation that theoretically belonged to the legislature.

As the number of special and local statutes increased (in 1873, of 1,119 statutes 1,034 were local or special in nature), so, too, did the demands for their prohibition. Several Civil War legislatures restricted the time devoted to such bills, and one governor vetoed several local statutes on the grounds that laws should apply equally to all counties, but until the Constitutional Convention of 1890, demands for more comprehensive reform came to naught. Feeling that their constituents almost unanimously desired basic change, the delegates to the convention outlawed most local and special legislation, causing future statute books to decrease markedly in size and future legislatures to have more time for the problems of the state as a whole.

But local legislation was only one of several problems afflicting county government. Under the system that prevailed until 1850, county courts were not only undemocratic but disorderly, inattentive, cumbersome, and inexpert. A majority of the justices of the peace had to be in attendance when major business was conducted, and courts found it difficult to muster quorums. In Barren County, a tavern owner had to wait eight months before a court could round up enough justices to hear his petition for a new license. Some courts fined members for absence without cause (and one went so far as to advertise for its missing members to appear), but most tolerated even the grossest negligence. While circuit courts had some authority to punish justices who failed to attend to court business, commonwealth attorneys seldom initiated action.

The steady expansion of the membership of the county courts in the first half of the century contributed to the cumbersomeness of the tribunals. A typical court session produced scenes of "confusion and disorder." Justices wandered in and out of the courtroom, sitting for only portions of cases. Sometimes when an even number of justices voted on specific issues, evenly split decisions would follow, with more indecision. Individual legislators introduced bills to cope with the problems, but the General Assembly refused to enact them. While some courts issued formal rules of order and procedure, most tolerated extreme informality bordering on chaos. A foreign visitor to an early nineteenth-century courtroom condemned the "wrangling and disputing" lawyers, the "clamorous" litigants, the "pertinacious and contemptuous" witnesses, and the "curious," "drunk," "laughing," and "shouting" spectators.

Most of the justices of the peace under the old court system lacked legal training, and despite their relatively high socioeconomic status, they refused to devote the time necessary to master the nuances of the legal specialties within their collective jurisdiction. Because of this lack of dedication, the record of the local tribunals upon review too often revealed numerous blunders. Observers especially castigated the courts for their execution of the probate laws, accusing the justices of negligence and even fraud.

Almost from the beginning of statehood in 1792, reformers demanded changes in the old county court system. In 1794, a correspondent to the *Kentucky Gazette* denounced the "petty tyrants" on the courts whose combination of powers served only the interests of the aristoc-

74

racy and not those of the people. On the eve of the Constitutional Convention of 1799, some protested the ability of justices of the peace to sit in the legislature and write the laws they would later enforce as individual magistrates and members of the county courts. "Why shall we suffer them to lord it over us with the pre-eminence of such dangerous, complicated and extensive powers?" asked another of the *Gazette*'s correspondents.

Despite these complaints and others, the county courts and county government in general emerged stronger than ever from the Constitutional Convention of 1799 which drafted the commonwealth's second constitution. The delegates converted the sheriffalty, which had been an elective office, to one firmly under the control of the county court. They did not prohibit justices of the peace from sitting in the General Assembly, and large numbers of them continued to do so during the early decades of the nineteenth century.

Added to the problems of cumbersomeness, inattentiveness, disorderliness, and inexpertness, the emergence of the first two-party system in Kentucky placed immense strains on the old county court system. Politicians successful at the ballot box were not always able to penetrate the closed quarters of county government. Many of these were Whig politicians from counties that voted Whig consistently but maintained Democratic county courts because of the constitutional guarantees of self-perpetuation. Whig frustrations at being closed out of many county governments, along with a growing split in their party, presented the Democrats (frustrated by their proscription from many state offices) with enough leverage to secure a referendum on the question of another constitutional convention in 1847 and 1848. County court gangs rallied in defense of the old constitution, but despite their intense efforts, Kentuckians overwhelmingly endorsed a convention call for 1849. During the campaign to elect delegates it became apparent that the old court system was a principal issue. Most candidates demanded changes, and the few who defended the status quo suffered overwhelming defeat.

The delegates to the Constitutional Convention of 1849 converted county government from one of self-perpetuation to what was essentially a democratic institution. Voters would thereafter elect all county officers for limited terms. Seeking to eliminate the awkwardness of the county court, the framers of Kentucky's third constitution created the office of county judge to perform the functions of the old county court except for those relating to its fiscal responsibilities.

Other than opening up county government to greater numbers of aspiring politicians, it is questionable whether the reformers of 1849 accomplished much in their new charter for the commonwealth. The reformers had failed to address themselves to many of the basic problems of the counties. Officers continued to be paid primarily from fees, and fee-gouging continued to plague the citizenry. Elected officials did not seem to perform any more competently than appointed ones, although the new office of county judge did bring some semblance of order to county court proceedings.

Above all else, the reformers of 1849 did not come to grips with the excessive number of counties in the commonwealth. Although nineteenth-century legislatures did not create as many counties after 1849 as had been established before that date, they nonetheless added nineteen to the already staggering number of one hundred. Increasingly, critics began to write and speak of "pauper counties"—those that received more state revenue than they produced. At first such a description fit counties mostly in eastern and southeastern Kentucky, but by 1890 it applied to nearly two-thirds of the state's local governments. In marked contrast, a handful of urban and Bluegrass counties, such as Jefferson, Kenton, Campbell, Fayette, Bourbon, Shelby, Scott, and Woodford counties, contributed 80 percent of the net revenue that went into the state treasury.

Many perceived a direct connection between the number of Kentucky counties and county poverty. Counties with small populations often found it difficult to elect qualified public officials. Critics noted that the abundance of counties produced the need for more local juries, contributed to the state's high crime rate, and caused many areas to go without needed improvements in transportation. The incompetence of county officials often led to inadequate tax assessment and collection and poor fiscal management. Smaller counties meant smaller tax bases, a serious handicap in an age of limited state and federal economic assistance.

As the number of pauper counties multiplied, so did calls for their abolition. Seldom did such propositions reach the legislature, and when they did they usually perished in committee, although the General Assembly nearly abolished Rowan County in 1888. Cynics speculated that the county escaped annihilation only because its partial merger with neighboring Fleming County would have reduced the strength of the state's dominant Democratic party.

Newspaper editors especially desired the consolidation of counties. Writing in 1871, the editor of the *Maysville Bulletin* proposed the abolition of all counties created since 1845 — or at least a permanent stop to the creation of new counties. In the journalist's opinion, government in many of the smaller counties had become "a ridiculous farce" because there were too few intelligent and competent men to run local affairs. In one instance, the editor reported, a healthy county with many bridges and turnpikes had given birth to several new counties whose smaller tax bases could not support macadamized roads or maintain routine services without state subsidies. The editor of the *Kentucky Gazette* advanced another formula for dealing with surplus counties. "Each and every county that has through a course of years proven itself incapable of supporting itself ought to be consolidated with another county and, if the new county still proves unable to take care of itself, let consolidation go on until they do become self sustaining."

The nineteenth-century movement to consolidate counties reached its height at the Constitutional Convention of 1890–1891. Delegates seriously debated the question, some asserting that the people demanded restrictions on the formation of new counties and even the abolition of existing ones, while others argued that many areas desired to add themselves to the growing number of counties. Kentucky's love affair with counties was highlighted by the contention of some delegates that the state lacked the power to merge counties, a proposition contradicting the leading national authorities on the subject. Although the reformers did not abolish any counties, they did provide for the possibility by granting such power to future legislatures. Furthermore, the convention voted to impose restrictions on the formation of additional counties.

The constitutional convention addressed itself to other problems of county government. The delegates imposed debt limitations on the counties, many of which had plunged into bankruptcy during the railroad craze of the previous forty years. They gave to future legislatures the option of abolishing the assessorship and of merging the office of commonwealth's attorney with the county attorney's office and the jailership with the sheriffalty. Counties also were given the option of adopting the commission form of government.

Despite these reforms, convention delegates left the county system largely intact. The fee system prevailed, except in Jefferson County, and continued to plague the performance of county officials. Experts studying county government in the 1920s and 1930s called for the abolition of the fee system, asserting that it caused county officials to take a proprietary attitude toward their positions. Although the legislature refused to heed the calls for reform, it did place limitations on the compensation of county officers by a law providing that surplus fees should go to the fiscal courts. But some county officials reportedly ignored this provision, and the state seemingly lacked sufficient employees and funds to enforce it.

Nor did the reformers remedy the headless structure of county government. No officer possessed the power to direct the over-all policy of county government. Twentieth-century commentators began to expose the problem but achieved no changes. While certain officials in some counties might become de facto leaders of their local government, their influence was usually only political in nature and temporary in duration.

Beset by the debilitating influence of the fee system and the absence of supervisory control, county officers continued to perform their official duties inconsistently. Some sheriffs still neglected the enforcement of criminal laws from either negligence or lack of funds while others performed remarkably, although they were shorthanded and underfunded. An observer noted in 1923 that the sheriff of Ohio County was "not interested in serving warrants of any kind, either civil or criminal . . . ; [his] chief interest is in collecting taxes." Other sheriffs performed in like manner, especially neglecting the enforcement of prohibition laws. Similar conditions prevailed in the 1930s, according to another commentator, who advocated the establishment of a state police force to augment county law enforcement. Responding to this and other such calls, the legislature finally created a state police department in 1948. After World War II some urban counties created separate county police forces, but most continued to rely on the sheriff as their principal policeman. Lack of funds made it difficult for some sheriffs to patrol their counties adequately. In 1974, the sheriff of Edmonson County donated most of his personal fees to

79

provide his county with twenty-four-hour protection, but despite his charity, voters overwhelmingly rejected a special tax which would have provided a permanent source of funds for law enforcement. State-wide, legislators and voters contributed to the problem by refusing to vote increases in compensation and rejecting a constitutional amendment allowing sheriffs to serve successive terms.

Continuing the decline that began with the reforms of 1849–1850, justices of the peace had fallen to a level of general judicial incompetence by the twentieth century. Fortunately for Kentucky's litigants, most ceased to perform judicial functions by the 1920s, confining themselves to the affairs of fiscal courts where they performed more ably. In 1975, Kentuckians achieved a major reform when they ratified a constitutional amendment stripping the justices and county judges of their judicial duties and transferring these responsibilities to newly created district judges trained in the law.

At least in the first part of the twentieth century, other county officers remained bogged down in fee gouging, conflict of interests, and neglect of duty. County attorneys sometimes represented clients whom they should have been prosecuting, or refused to investigate or prosecute suspected wrongdoers because they were "friends." In 1923, citing the county attorneys' general lack of knowledge of the fundamentals of the law, the attorney general unavailingly called for the merger of the county attorney's office with that of the commonwealth's attorney and the creation of a special task force to oversee prosecutions in certain of the counties.

Other nineteenth-century problems persisted. Jailers found it difficult to maintain secure jails. County courts continued to sell treasuryships in violation of the law. Claims processing continued to be arbitrary until generally effective reforms were undertaken in the 1930s. Tax assessment and collection continued to be unfair. Reforms corrected abuses here, too, although some critics denied the efficacy of the changes. Debt limitations did not prevent many counties from repudiating bonds during the Depression. Gradually throughout the twentieth century, counties relinquished to the state their control over roads, and what jurisdiction they retained was strengthened by more modern approaches to maintenance.

With the Depression and the need for fiscal retrenchment, reformers renewed their calls for county consolidation. In 1931, Professor John W. Manning, a political scientist at the University of Kentucky, argued that counties were obsolete in an age of sophisticated transportation and communication and called for the reduction of their number in Kentucky from 120 to 20. Such a move, Manning contended, would save the taxpayers over $2,500,000 per year as well as rid the state of many "misfit uniformities" which applied to rural and urban sections alike. Impressed by Manning's logic, the state's most influential newspaper, the *Louisville Courier-Journal*, enthusiastically supported his proposals, noting that consolidation would eliminate many useless jobs and duplications of services. The *Courier-Journal* also predicted that merger would seriously weaken the county political machines which, in its opinion, accounted "for practically every evil in [state] government from inequality of representation to inequality of taxation."

Others rallied to support Manning's proposal, including the state official most acquainted with the realities of county finances, the Inspector and Examiner. The proposal elicited a lively debate in the *Courier-Journal*'s letters to the editor, with most writers supporting consolidation. One irate correspondent submitted that merger would reduce the number of government officials—"largely the cause of our mental distress and our financial decay." Several other newspapers joined the *Courier-Journal*'s campaign.

Despite their early initiative and the logic of their demands, reformers found themselves outnumbered and outmaneuvered by supporters of the status quo. Rather than save Kentuckians' tax dollars, stand-patters argued, consolidation would increase expenditures, since new courthouses would have to be built to accommodate larger counties, and county residents would have to spend more for transportation to remote county seats. Some even raised the nineteenth-century specter of general lawlessness should large numbers of counties be eliminated; they asserted that such a change would make law enforcement much more difficult. Others predicted the collapse of the economies of towns whose status as county seats would be wiped out by consolidation.

More important than these arguments was the political power of the stand-patters. "One hundred twenty entrenched courthouse cliques, and their families and friends" formed the nucleus of political opposition to any change in county boundaries. Often derived from these cliques and usually dependent upon them in large degree for reelection and political support, legislators and administrators in Frankfort feared the consequences if they tampered with local tradition. County newspapers, often the beneficiaries of profitable county printing contracts, opposed consolidation out of self-interest. Undergirding the opposition to reform were hundreds of thousands of rural Kentuckians who derived special pride from their spirited loyalty to their counties.

Confronted with intense lobbying by county officials and their allies, and beset with their own insecurities, legislators quickly rejected all attempts at consolidation in the 1930s and thereafter. The Constitutional Revision Assembly of 1964–1966 actually made consolidation more difficult in their proposed new constitution. Even so, courthouse gangs, fearful of any change that might remotely threaten their bastions, led the successful fight against the new charter, which was buried at the polls in 1966. In a rare departure from the general trend against change, Fayette County merged with the city of Lexington in 1974, after voters solidly supported consolidation; but one year later voters in Boyd County overwhelmingly rejected a proposed merger of the governments of Ashland and Catlettsburg with that of the county.

Kentucky is not the only state with an antiquated system of local government. County structures in almost every other state contain outdated and useless institutional devices and personnel. And in other states, too, reformers have largely failed. Instead, the national trend is toward a proliferation of local governmental units. In 1966, the Committee for Improvement of Management in Government reported that there were more than 80,000 such units, including over 3,000 counties and more than twenty times as many special districts. Of these local units, in the words of an early twentieth-century expert, the county remains the "dark continent of American politics." Dark though it may be, the county reigns supreme in Kentucky.

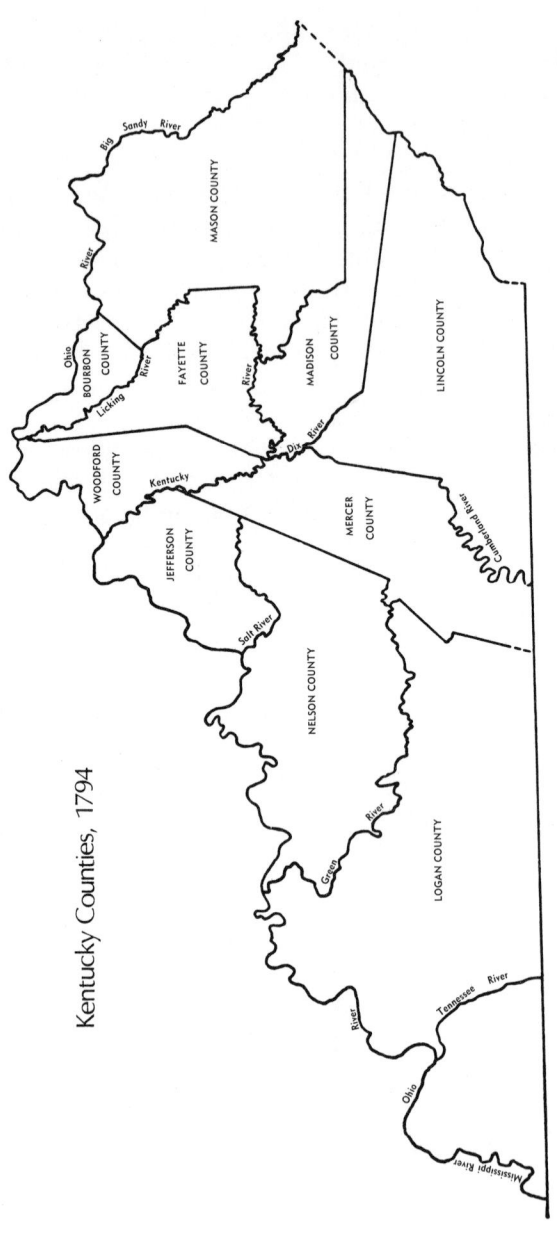

Kentucky Counties, 1794

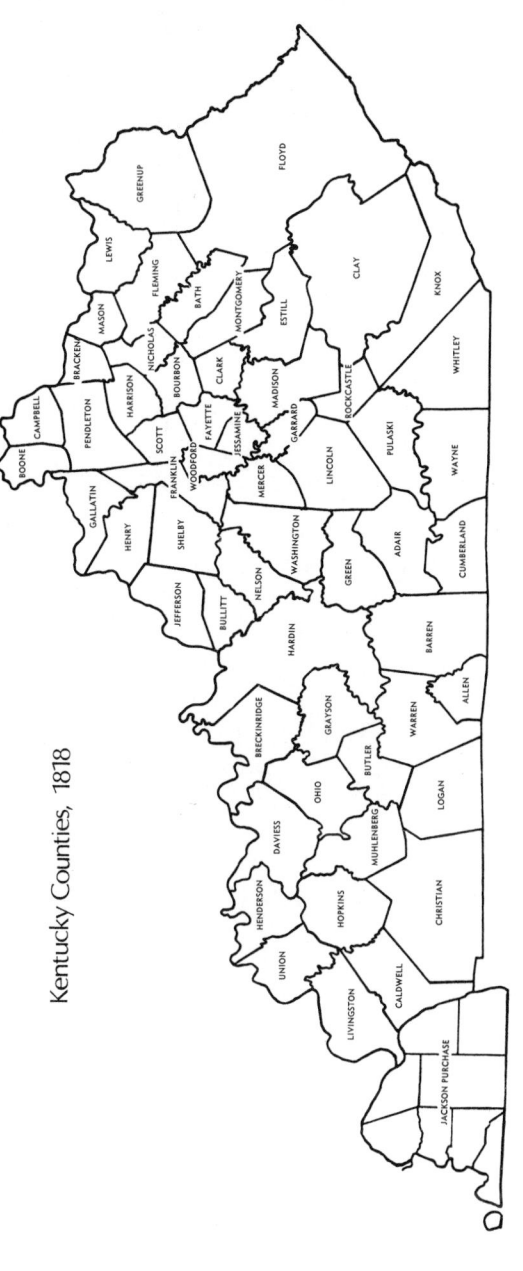

Kentucky Counties, 1818

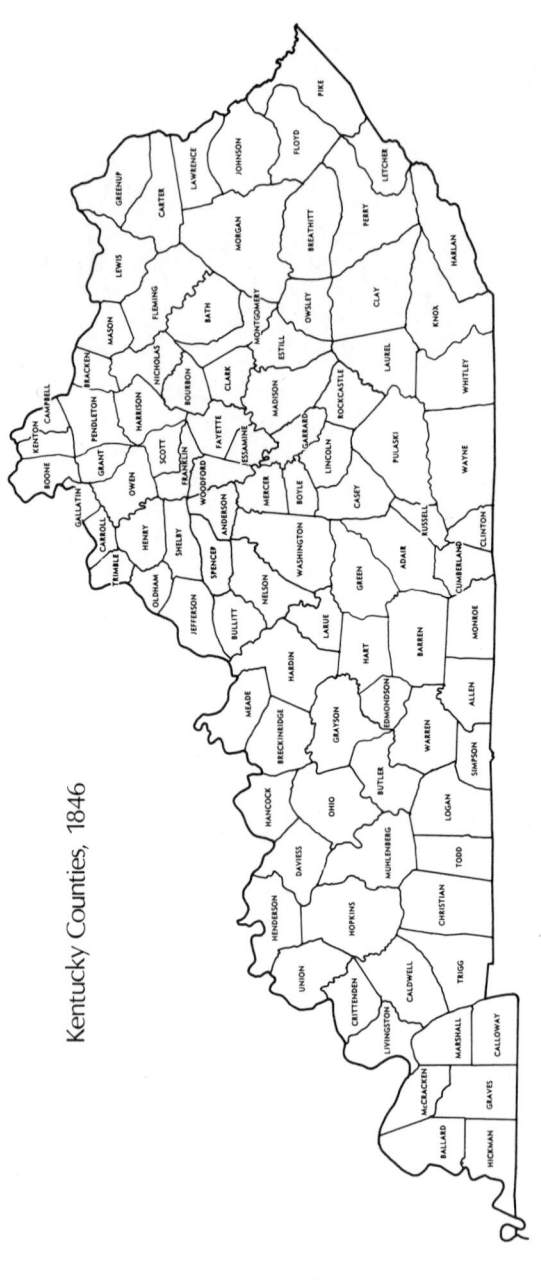

Kentucky Counties, 1846

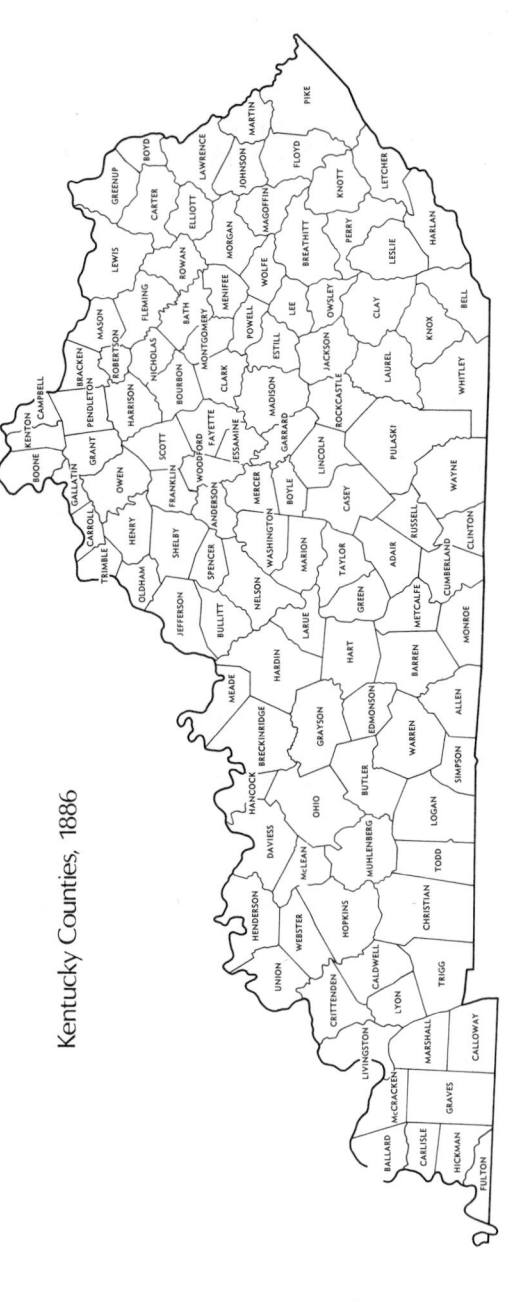

Kentucky Counties, 1886

Bibliographical Essay

AMONG THE fundamental sources of information on Kentucky's counties are the order and minute books of the county courts. These books contain summaries of the business of the county courts. All are handwritten for the nineteenth century, most are legible, and some contain indexes. Originals of these books may be found either in the county seat or at the State Archives and Records Service in Frankfort. Microfilm of many of the nineteenth-century records is available at King Library, Special Collections, University of Kentucky.

Especially valuable for the politics of county government before 1851 are the Papers of the Governors of Kentucky, located at the Kentucky Historical Society in Frankfort and available there also in microfilm. For a generally reliable guide to these papers see Emma Guy Cromwell's *A Catalogue of the Records, Documents, Papers . . . of the Governors of Kentucky, 1792–1926* (Frankfort, Ky., 1926). Among the most relevant papers are the journals and letterbooks of the governors, the registers of justices of the peace, lists of justices of the peace for particular years, and letters, petitions, recommendations, and other documents relating to county officers.

The *Acts of Kentucky,* the *Journals of the House of Representatives,* and the *Journals of the Senate* are rich in information about the counties. They contain much proposed and finished legislation about the local units of government. Also valuable are the *Kentucky Documents* and the four constitutions of Kentucky. To supplement the *Acts,* one should consult William Waller Hening's

The Statutes at Large: Being a Collection of All the Laws of Virginia, 1619–1792, 13 vols. (New York and Philadelphia, 1819–1823); William Littell's *The Statute Law of Kentucky with Notes, Praelections, and Observations on the Public Acts* . . . , 5 vols. (Frankfort, Ky., 1809–1819); Littell and Jacob Swigert's *A Digest of the Statute Law of Kentucky: Being a Collection of All the Acts of the General Assembly* . . . , 2 vols. (Frankfort, Ky., 1822); C. S. Morehead and Mason Brown's *A Digest of the Statute Laws of Kentucky of a Public and Permanent Nature* . . . , 2 vols. (Frankfort, Ky., 1834); Preston S. Loughborough's *Kentucky Laws, Statutes . . . of a Public and Permanent Nature Passed since 1834* (Frankfort, Ky., 1842); Richard H. Stanton's *The Revised Statutes of Kentucky* . . . , 2 vols. (Cincinnati, O., 1860); Harvey Myers's *A Digest of the General Laws of Kentucky* . . . (Frankfort, Ky., 1866); Joshua F. Bullitt and John Feland's *The General Statutes of Kentucky* (Frankfort, Ky., 1877); and Bullitt and Feland's *The General Statutes of Kentucky* (Louisville, Ky., 1888).

Delegates to Kentucky's two constitutional conventions of the nineteenth century spoke fully and freely about the realities of Kentucky's counties and their governments. Their comments may be found in the *Report of the Debates and Proceedings of the Convention for the Revision of the Constitution of the State of Kentucky, 1849* (Frankfort, Ky., 1849) and *Official Report of the Proceedings and Debates in the Convention . . . of . . . 1890 to Adopt, Amend, or Change the Constitution of the State of Kentucky*, 4 vols. (Frankfort, Ky., 1890).

Containing summaries of controversies affecting the counties and important insights into their internal workings are the printed reports of the Court of Appeals found in the *Kentucky Reports*, the *Kentucky Law Reporter*, and *Kentucky Opinions*. Relevant cases are digested in Benjamin Moore and James Harlan's *Digest of Cases at Common Law and in Equity Decided by the Court of*

Appeals of Kentucky . . . *1792 to 1853,* 2 vols. (Frankfort, Ky., 1853) and Joseph Barbour's *Kentucky Digest* . . . , 4 vols. (Louisville, Ky., 1878–1897). Federal courts sometimes heard important cases about the counties. For these consult *Federal Cases,* the *United States Reports,* and the Federal Circuit Court Order Books in the Federal Archives and Records Center in Chicago.

Students of Kentucky's counties in the nineteenth century should also investigate William B. Allen's *Kentucky Officer's Guide and Legal Hand-Book* . . . (Louisville, Ky., 1860); Richard H. Stanton's *A Practical Treatise on the . . . Powers and Duties of Justices of the Peace (etc.)* . . . (Cincinnati, O., 1875); Lewis N. Dembitz's *Kentucky Jurisprudence* (Louisville, Ky., 1890); and Robert M. Bradley's satirical *A Sketch of Granny Short's Barbecue and the General Statutes of Kentucky* (Louisville, Ky., 1879).

Crucial to an understanding of the counties during the Civil War and Reconstruction are the *War of the Rebellion: Official Records of the Union and Confederate Armies,* four series, 128 vols. (Washington, D.C., 1880–1901) and Freedmen's Bureau Records, Record Group 105 in the National Archives and Records Service, Washington, D.C.

Kentucky's newspapers form a treasure trove of information about the counties. Among the most revelant are the *Kentucky Gazette, Kentucky Reporter, Observer and Reporter, Intelligencer, Daily Press, Weekly Press, Kentucky Statesman, Leader, Herald,* and *Transcript* (all of Lexington); Frankfort's *Palladium, Argus of Western America, Commonwealth, Kentucky Yeoman, Convention, Capital,* and *Roundabout;* Louisville's *Public Advertiser, Daily Journal, Courier, Daily Focus, Evening Post, Daily Democrat,* and *Courier-Journal;* the *Western Citizen* and *True Kentuckian* of Paris; the *Bulletin* and *Republican* of Maysville; and the *Barbourville Mountain Echo, London Mountain Echo, Robertson County Tri-*

bune, Stanford Interior Journal, Hickman Courier, Falmouth Independent, Cynthiana News, Georgetown Weekly Times, Winchester Sun, Kentucky Tribune, and *Bardstown Herald.* The *New York Times* is also informative.

Useful manuscript collections include the Mason County Historical Papers (microfilm), the Martin Cox Papers (microfilm), the Brutus Clay Papers (microfilm), the Perry Family Papers, and the John Whyte Stevenson Papers, all in King Library, Special Collections, University of Kentucky; and the Joseph Hamilton Daveiss Papers and the Orlando Brown Papers, both at the Filson Club in Louisville.

On Kentucky generally, one should consult Humphrey Marshall's *History of Kentucky,* 2d ed., 2 vols. (Frankfort, Ky., 1824); Lewis and Richard H. Collins's *History of Kentucky,* 2 vols. (Covington, Ky., 1874); and especially Thomas D. Clark's *Kentucky: Land of Contrasts* (New York, 1968). On the counties generally, see Robert M. Ireland's *The County Courts in Antebellum Kentucky* (Lexington, Ky., 1972) and *Little Kingdoms: The Counties of Kentucky, 1850–1891* (Lexington, Ky., to be published). See also B. O. Gaines's *History of Scott County,* 2 vols. (Georgetown, Ky., 1906) and Otto A. Rothert's *A History of Muhlenberg County* (Louisville, Ky., 1913), the latter containing a summary of the Muhlenberg County railroad debt war. For modern county problems, see H. S. Gilbertson, *County Government in Kentucky: A Report by the Efficiency Commission of Kentucky* (Frankfort, Ky., 1923); John W. Manning, *The Government of Kentucky* (Lexington, Ky., 1938); Henry C. Pepper, "County Government in Kentucky," (typescript in King Library, ca. 1938); and Kenneth E. Vanlandingham, *The Constitution and Local Government,* Kentucky Legislative Research Commission Informational Bulletin no. 36 (1964).

Studies containing useful information on particular aspects of Kentucky's counties include Basil W. Duke,

The Commercial and Railroad Development of Kentucky (Frankfort, Ky., 1887); L. L. Robinson, *Railroad Statistics: . . . to the Voters of Mason County* (Maysville, Ky., 1850); William C. Ireland, *Elizabethtown, Lexington, & Big Sandy R.R. . . . : In Opposition to the Proposed Subscription* (Ashland, Ky., 1871); James Lane Allen, "County Court Day in Kentucky," *Harper's Magazine* 79 (August 1889): 383–97; W. C. McChord, *Report on the Financial Condition of Washington County* (Lebanon, Ky., 1879); Charles Chauncy Binney, "Restrictions on Special and Local Legislation," *American Law Register*, n.s. 32 (1894): 613–32, 721–45, 816–57, 922–43, 1019–33, 1109–61; Lyman H. Cloe and Sumner Marcus, "Special and Local Legislation," *Kentucky Law Journal* 24 (May 1936): 349–86; E. Merton Coulter, *Civil War and Readjustment in Kentucky* (Chapel Hill, N.C., 1926); Allen W. Trelease, *White Terror: The Ku Klux Klan Conspiracy and Southern Reconstruction* (New York, 1971); Harold Wilson Coates, *Stories of Kentucky Feuds* (Knoxville, Tenn., 1923); Carl B. Boyd, Jr., "Local Aid to Railroads in Central Kentucky, 1850–1891" (master's thesis, University of Kentucky, 1963); Frank Mathias, "The Turbulent Years of Kentucky Politics, 1820–1850" (Ph.D. diss., University of Kentucky, 1966); Carl R. Field, "The Making of Kentucky's Third Constitution" (Ph.D. diss., University of Kentucky, 1951); Leonard P. Curry, "Election Year: Kentucky, 1828," *Register, Kentucky Historical Society* 55 (July 1957): 196–212; and Jasper B. Shannon and Ruth McQuown, *Presidential Politics in Kentucky, 1824–1948* (Lexington, Ky., 1950).